Robert B. Mellor

Innovation
Management

Forlaget Globe 2003

- the short road to knowledge

Innovation Management

Copyright
2003 © by Forlaget Globe A/S
1. edition, 1. printing

Publisher

Forlaget Globe A/S
Skodsborgvej 305
DK-2850 Nærum
Tlf. +45 70 15 14 00
Fax +45 70 15 14 10
E-mail: info@globe.dk
URL:http://www.globe.dk

Author
Robert B. Mellor

Editor
Carsten Straaberg
(redaktion@globe.dk)

Cover
Per Schou

DtP
Carsten Straaberg

Printed by BookPartner A/S, Denmark

Printed in Denmark 2003

ISBN 87-7900-196-3

Innovation Management

By Robert B. Mellor, D.Sc., MBA

Dr. Robert B. Mellor lectures both at the Copenhagen Business School and at the IT University of Copenhagen. He is expert advisor to the European Commission, has over 17 years university teaching experience and is examiner at several universities all over the world. He is author of over 100 research publications in journals including Nature, and has written several books on computer programming, and on e-business.

Contents

Contents 4

Foreword 5

1. Innovation throughout history...6

2. Incentives for innovation. 9

3. What is entrepreneurship?...11

4. Entrepreneurship in a macroeconomic context..15

5. Creativity..18

6. The Computer Revolution...23

7. The IT industry 25

8. Innovative enterprises. 27

9. The psychological wringer..31

10. The investor chain...34

11. Types of investment..39

12. Setting up the company...44

13. The strategic business proposition. 47

14. Marketing plan..52

15. Business plan 63

16. Attracting attention. 70

17. Encouraging entrepreneurial spin-offs...79

18. Literature...84

19. Appendix A: R U E-Ready? 88

20. Index. 93

Foreword

I started teaching the course "Innovation Management - from Idea to Growth", at the IT University of Copenhagen in the year 2000. At that time it seemed like anyone who scribbled something containing the word "Internet" on the back of an envelope, could cash it in for millions. Despite the NASDAQ crash and recession, I still see all around me that the good ideas, when properly worked through, still get the support and investment they need. However what the entrepreneur (and especially the young technical entrepreneur) needs, is to find out how to get their idea polished up to the required standard. I even find it positive when the individual can see that his/her idea was not quite up to standard, since it shows that they have acquired a good degree of insight.

A simple push-pull model serves to remind us that both good ideas and a market for them, are essential for the success of any innovatory activity. However, push does not automatically connect to pull. Thus inventive ability, technological capacity and need (social demand) have to be synchronized so that neither pre-maturity, nor delay, can inhibit innovation and entrepreneurship. This book points to how this can be achieved, but it is not a cookbook with recipes for success, rather tried and tested course material. However experience shows that it is extremely comprehensible (participants regularly evaluated the above course as "excellent") and practical. Indeed many participants have subsequently successfully set up high-tech (and low-tech) companies. Despite this, perhaps the real value lies amongst those participants who have not yet started their own company. Perhaps these are prepared minds, waiting receptively for chance's favor.

1. Innovation throughout history.

The development of highly sophisticated cultures depends on two phases. Firstly, the food supply must grow. As soon as the food supply is sufficient, that people don't have to scratch their living from the soil every day, then they can experiment with things in their environment.

The second phase is social mobility, perhaps protected by laws and customs, which make positive innovation possible.

By 8000 BC, humans had begun to use agriculture, as opposed to being purely hunter-gatherers. For the first time people were able to use relatively permanent settlements, and this, together with the greater productivity of their efforts, enabled them to devote more time to non-subsistence activities. As population grows, more hands are available for labor tasks and, as Adam Smith pointed out, division of labor involves specialization. Specialization leads to greater efficiency and technological progress. Indeed pottery, requiring less labor to produce than stone containers, was in use around 2000 years later. However hunting, gathering and farming were complementary activities for many generations. Perhaps migratory bands or hunting expeditions would replace shelters of skins and tree branches with dugouts or wooden shelters, followed by sod houses and eventually houses of sun-dried mud brick. Experience in making bricks may have been cross-fertilized with pottery skills. As potters refined their art, they invented the potters' wheel, preceding the use of the wheel for transport.

Such invention and innovation progressed by almost-imperceptible increments. This type of progress is thus called "incremental innovation". In spreading from village to village and from farmer to farmer, we can also speak of "horizontal innovation". In this situation, innovation is spread between peers, i.e. people with common problems, and without large differences in social status, caste etc.

Going hand-in-hand with incremental innovation is radical innovation, and with horizontal innovation, vertical innovation. Radical innovation is an intellectual jump, which changes a whole area. An example of this is the steam engine of the 1770s, which revolutionized industrial production, the price of cotton cloth fell to 0.1% of what it had been. Vertical innovation reflects the mobility of ideas between the social strata of a society. Paradoxically, to illustrate what vertical innovation is, it is best to take an example where it was lacking.

The peak of the classical civilization was the Roman Empire. The city of Rome itself may have had one million inhabitants at its height, a feat not repeated until 2000 years later in London. Roman society was highly stratified, with the nobility dedicating themselves to leisure and religion, and their sons to the arts of war. Roman roads stretched from the Caspian Sea in the east, to present-day Portugal and Britain. However these roads were used for communication by messenger and for strategic use (chariots and armies), but hardly for commercial traffic. Commerce was left to inferior classes (even foreigners). Great progress was made in philosophy, mathematics and art, but not in the applications of science, e.g. steam-powered trinkets, the waterwheel and the windmill had all been invented by 100 AD. But Roman ingenuity manifested itself in roads, aqueducts and domed buildings, not in laborsaving machines. The nobility was well able to design advanced works as an intellectual exercise, but they lacked both the experience and inclination to experiment with the means of production, because labor carried the stigma of menial status. Slaves did the productive work. But even if the slave class had had any opportunity to improve technology, they would have reaped few (if any) benefits from their inventions, either in terms of higher incomes, or as reduced labor. The decline of the Roman Empire was probably due to this lack of technological creativity.

This lack of incentive for the slave laboring class, and thus lack of vertical innovation, is the reason why societies based on slavery may produce art or literature (which may even be considered to be radical innovation), but such a society cannot produce sustained economic or technological growth.

This is in sharp contrast to today's Internet world, where high degrees of anonymity rule, often you don't know if the person you are talking to is black, white, old, young, male or female. All barriers are down and everyone is equal. And those straight and wide Roman roads are now optical backbone connections, carrying millions of dollars of value every minute.

The degree of progress in society is dependent on the ability of its members to think rationally. Discovery started as a rationalization of myth, for example the rationality expressed by William of Occam, (a British intellectual in Köln between ca 1300-1350). Britain's liberal immigration policy, from around 1500, under the reign especially of Henry VIII, was a magnet in attracting those individuals who confronted intellectual, social and/or religious barriers elsewhere in Europe. The peak was in the late 1700s when the Industrial Revolution in Britain coincided with the 30 Years Embargo due to the Napoleonic Wars, leading to a refined industrial society needing only markets (selling opportunities) to expand explosively (incidentally leading to "gunboat diplomacy"). Compulsory universal education (from 1888) plus free university education (from 1945) kept Britain in high gear until the Second World War.

The enormous ecological and economical diversity of the USA has lead to enormous resource availability when needed. Especially WWII led to principal discoveries and enormous applications in the USA, especially in the area of management, e.g. the development and application of "just-in-time" management in relationship to D-Day.

Summary
Innovation is essential to development and human progress. Innovation builds on education and intellectual freedom.

2. Incentives for innovation.

There is a lot of hard work, disappointment and frustration involved in becoming a successful entrepreneur. Therefore one may ask; why do it? Surely there are 2 answers to this; personal and intellectual. However, before examining motivation, it should be said that entrepreneurship is psychological. There is a story of an American boy who had a father who was an academic. The boy was always told "do some good work and your boss will reward you with a step up the career ladder". On the other hand, the same boy knew the neighbor, who was a successful entrepreneur. The entrepreneur could not understand this theory of advancement at all. He simply recommended owning the ladder. This simple story illustrates that attitude may be inherited. Clearly some people, aristocracy etc., are born rich. Amongst the rest of humanity (the vast majority) some may have inherited a "loser" mentality. However it is up to the individual to decide which principles they wish to live their lives after.

Motivation to be an entrepreneur may be personal, you may like to make a lot of money. On the other hand it may be intellectual. For example you may like to analyze economy, business processes or science. Einstein started his work on relativity by imagining what things would look like if he traveled on a beam of light. When asked what single event was most helpful in developing the Theory of Relativity, Albert Einstein replied: "Figuring out how to think about the problem." Exactly this, figuring out the problem, is a large part of innovation. What is it the customers want, even when they don't know it themselves.

Discovery, invention and innovation have very different incentives. These differences also create difficulties in transfer from one activity to another. This is because the "cultures" are different. Thus further "mixing incentives" are required. These incentives build on complex underlying psychological phenomena. For example there are thousands of charitable or beneficial, non-profit and not-for-profit organizations around the world. Some of there are very large indeed, some are very innovative (e.g. the flying hospital, a converted jet airliner). Thus the following three categories do not provide a clear explanation which convincingly uncovers all forms of motivation, but which, however, covers most motivations.

Discovery: Fame brings scientists rewards. "Free publication rights" is a scientists reward system, (be "the expert" in area no one has ever heard of) but it promotes a free flow of ideas. When this gets mixed with other systems, conflict can result. Several state-paid scientists have become very rich, but other scientists say "I am a martyr to purity - just take my ideas".

Invention: There are 3 major forms of property; patents, copyright & trade secrets. Without these rights competitors would immediately copy your ideas, but without the initial costs, their "product" would always be cheaper, so taking up new ideas would always be economic suicide! During my job as R&D director of a German company it was my job to talk to academics with ideas. Some of these people were dedicated scientists, perhaps even brilliant. Thus it was a pity when they end their presentation with something like; "and the best part is that I haven't patented it, so you can just take it for free". Unfortunately they had not realized that all research costs might be 1% of a product, setting up production 10%, and marketing 89%. So why should there be such a large investment, when a competitor could simply headhunt a few key workers and make exactly the same product for a fraction of the cost. Unfortunately the most genial, brilliant invention, which could save humanity, will go unused if not patented. Fortunately incentives are being developed in this area, where license money from patents are fed back to the inventors research. Laws around IPR change with time (e.g. copyright originally covered books, but now also covers software).

There are no formal rights for simply achieving better performance. Thus imitators copy anything appearing promising. Innovation is measured by "benchmarking", i.e. the comparison of your performance with the rest of the world. This is good motivation for the ambitious.

Summary
On top of creativity and philanthropy, fame, property and ambition provide motivation and incentive for innovation.

3. What is entrepreneurship?

Discovery is a new addition to knowledge. These are (normally) in the physical, biological or social sciences. Theoretical knowledge is obtained from observations and experimental testing of hypotheses and practical knowledge from practice: e.g. the practical knowledge acquired by a workforce in making new machinery operate well.

Invention is a new device or process. Most inventionss are minor improvements and do not qualify as patents. To qualify as a patent an invention must a pass a test of originality (i.e. is different from previous inventions). Only a small percentage of patents have any economic value. Those that do tend to be those which are immediately applicable. An example of this is the Phillips screw (patented by the Dutch Phillips concern - and the Worlds most lucrative patent) which made two crosswise grooves in a screw head instead of only one. This screw can be gripped by robot arms, thus opening whole assembly lines to automation.

Innovation is a better way of doing things. An innovation improves performance in goal-directed behavior (e.g. re-election politics, personal lifestyle) as measured by a criterion (e.g. profit maximization).

Invention is NOT innovation. To understand this difference, think of spreadsheet programs like Excel. The invention is the computer and its various parts, including software. However using spreadsheets to plan hourly work in your office, is an innovation. Invention is promoted by discovery (esp. in biology) whereas innovation is promoted by invention (esp. in industrial engineering and business). As science advances it creates opportunities for new inventions. However to develop economic value, massive knowledge can be needed (e.g. modern airplanes needed the development of the whole science of aerodynamics).

For invention, intellectual property rights (IPR) apply. There are 3 major forms; patents, copyright & trade secrets. Without these rights competitors would immediately copy your ideas, but without the initial costs, their "product" would always be cheaper - so taking up new ideas would always be economic suicide! Laws around IPR change with time (e.g. copyright originally covered books, but now also covers software).

Innovation is often about better performance. Here there are no formal rights. Thus imitators copy anything appearing promising. Innovation is measured by "benchmarking" - comparison of your performance with the rest of the world. An extreme example of protecting an innovation is the trade secret. For example, all the ingredients used to make Coca-Cola have been known for many decades, but the exact formula for the drink was a closely guarded secret until recently.

In order to make a living today, especially on the Internet, you don't have to make a spectacular invention, or a revolutionary new innovation. Most companies are simply entrepreneurial. The word entrepreneur comes from the French "entre" meaning "between". The root of the verb entreprendre can be traced back to around 1200. By 1500 a noun form appeared and soon thereafter both the verb and noun entered the English language. Already in 1730 "entrepreneur" was used to mean a self-employed person with a tolerance for risk. Towards the beginning of the industrial revolution Jean-Baptiste Say further expanded this definition to include the possession of managerial skills. Today an entrepreneur means a middleman or go-between. The entrepreneur has simply had an idea about how to do things better, or how to position him/herself in a moneymaking process, and manage this process to a successful conclusion.

This can be illustrated by the following simple example. Company E offers training in computers and computer software (programs). Many other firms who wish to upgrade the skills their staff have, regularly send groups of their staff on such courses. Company E knows from experience that the trainees need a book about that subject that they are learning, but that if they simply recommend the book, then most of the trainees will turn up to lessons without it. Therefore Company E buys enough copies to give to the trainees, and simply puts the price of the book on the bill that the trainees' firm pays for the course. The books come from a publishing house in the USA (here called Publishers X). Firm P imports them, then puts on tax, and sells them at a profit to Company E. Employee T, in Company E, notices that Publisher X has recently started a scheme on the Internet, selling books in bulk at 40% discount. By buying on the Internet, T does not have the overheads that P has, so he can sell the books to E at a lower price than P can. By cutting out P as supplier, and using T instead, E can either pass on the savings to the end-customer, or absorb the increased profit. Either way, X, T and E are happy, and P has been cut out of the business (or at least the business of X's books to E).

This example illustrates entrepreneurship (T is the entrepreneur). It also illustrates the "value chain". The value chain is the inter-linked series of business events connected to the rising value of the books, from X (where they are relatively cheap), to the end-customer (where they are relatively expensive). The books rise in value as they pass along the value chain from X to T (or P) to E to the end-customer.

All change is a source of innovative opportunity. This includes:

- The unexpected
- The incongruity
- Process need
- Changes in industry or market structure
- Demographics
- Changes in perception, mood, meaning
- New knowledge

The example also illustrates another phenomenon, "creative destruction". Typically with the introduction of new technology (in the example, the Internet) a new business situation is created, by destroying the old. In this case P has suffered from creative destruction, it should have been faster to adopt new technology and thus cut overheads. However (luckily for the small entrepreneur) existing large firms are seldom capable of making major shifts in technology. For example, why did railroad firms not open automobile factories? The management of existing firms has invested enormous amounts of man-years in understanding their particular business whilst they have no expertise in the "new(er) technology". Their knowledge of the old prevented them from appreciating the new.

Entrepreneurship goes hand-in-hand with opportunity. To put it briefly:

- There are very few opportunities to create a new industry.
- There are more opportunities to create new services
- There are many opportunities to inhabit/create a new niche market

The Internet is full of opportunities for entrepreneurial action. However it should be understood that entrepreneurial action is typically short-lived. Its lifetime is exactly as long as it takes for the next entrepreneur to show up! One anecdote about entrepreneurship is from J.B. Fuqua, Chairman of Fuqua Industries Inc., who said, "What's the secret of entrepreneurial success? It's knowing how to use OPB (other people's brains) and OPM (other people's money)".

Summary
The entrepreneur takes advantage of the value chain to change a business environment. This innovative process often involves the creative destruction of the old process.

4. Entrepreneurship in a macroeconomic context

Adam Smith founded modern economics with the publication of "The Wealth of Nations" in 1776. Smith argued that market economies generally serve the public interest and that the state should therefore not interfere with the functioning of the economy. Another influential economist was Thomas Malthus (1766-1834) who argued that population growth would lead to starvation, and that this starvation would be most spread amongst the least successful, i.e. the lower class. However several economists pointed out that there was food enough, but that the lower classes lacked the means to pay for it. Prominent amongst the opposition to Malthus was David Ricardo (1772-1823), who argued that unemployment was the result of wages being too high. Ricardo was supported by Jean-Baptiste Say (1776-1832), who stated that general overproduction and prolonged unemployment were impossible. Indeed "Say's Law" states that "supply creates its own demand", or that the production of goods generates sufficient income to ensure that goods are sold. John Maynard Keynes (1883-1946) later argued, like Malthus, that unemployment was primarily due to failure of demand. However he reasoned that the state should intervene by increasing spending in times of slump. This view prevailed until the 1970s, when both unemployment and inflation were increasing and the management of demand policies seemed to have no answer. At this time focus switched to supply and the role of money. Monetarism is primarily associated with Milton Friedman, who looked back at the quantity theory of money. The quantity theory of money is at least 500 years old (indeed some suggest it began with the Chinese philosopher Confucius - born 551 BC). The theory states that changes in the money supply lead to changes in price levels and wages, but have no effect on output and employment:

$$MV=PY$$

Where M stands for money supply, V for the velocity of circulation, P for price levels and Y for real output. Thus if money circulates quickly, less will be needed to sustain price levels. However if V is constant, then changes in M will affect P. Thus the quantity theory of money is also the theory of inflation.

Amongst these mainstream theories, the role of entrepreneurship received relatively little research and was rather overlooked. This is probably because it is not amenable to mathematical modeling. However entrepreneurship theory and practice was introduced by Joseph

Schlumpeter. Schumpeter is credited with many significant developments in economic theory, including the notion of "perfect competition" in an infinite marketplace. However Schlumpeters book "Theorie der wirtschaftlichen Entwicklung" (1912) directed the attention of economists away from static systems and towards economic advancement. Schlumpeter believed that the innovation practiced by entrepreneurs allows economic systems to avoid repetition, especially repetition of old mistakes, and thus progress to more advanced states. Schumpeter also popularized the work of Nikolai Kondratieff. Kondratieff developed the theory that technology stimulates industries in waves lasting approximately 50 years (the Kondratieff Cycle), consisting of around 20 years to perfect and use a series of related technologies, followed by 20 years where the growth industries appear to be doing well, but what looks like record profits are actually repayments on capital in industries that have ceased to grow. This perilous situation can turn to crisis, often precipitated by a relatively minor panic, and crash. There follows a long period of stagnation during which new, emergent technologies cannot generate enough jobs to make the economy grow again. Completed Kondratieff Cycles include the "steam/agriculture" cycle (1820-1870), "rail/coal/textile" cycle (1870-1930) and the "auto/rubber/petroleum" cycle (1930-1980). Kondratieff also predicted that the content of previous cycles cannot be repeated, thus earning himself execution at the hands of Stalin, who had just instigated an "agricultural reform" in the USSR.

However Schlumpeter and Kondratieff may still have gone unnoticed if it had not been for the works of Peter Drucker. In the text "Innovation and Entrepreneurship" (1985) Drucker contrasts the employment situation in Europe and in the USA. The USA was booming whilst Europe showed the symptoms of being at the stagnation end of a Kondratieff cycle. Drucker argued that the difference was due to the entrepreneurial culture in the USA. The effect was that within 5 years most European governments (and the EU) had passed legislation setting up initiatives to promote innovation and entrepreneurship.

It should, however, be noted that Drucker does not see IT, especially in the USA, as being the start of a new Kondratieff cycle. Drucker notes that actually few jobs are created in "high tech" firms, and rather that IT is an enabling technology, making it possible for Small and Medium-sized Enterprises (SMEs) in a range of different branches to profitably exploit niches which otherwise may not be profitable. It has been estimated that, in the west, SMEs are responsible for creating around 70% of all jobs and indeed represent the most efficient use of economic resources.

Thus the content of the next Kondratieff cycle is unknown, but guesses include nano-electronics, space technology and bioengineering.

Summary
Innovation and entrepreneurship are hard to model and thus hard to predict. However they make up a large part of the economy.

5. Creativity.

Invention is the process of discovering a principle, design is the process of incorporating the principle, and innovation is the application of the principle. All of these are embodiments of creativity. Probably everyone is creative, some have high potential, and some have lower potential. Many psychologists believe that most of us use only between five and ten percent of our potential. The main reason why most of the potential is "lost", is the individual's attitude. The environment in turn, often forms this attitude and unfortunately most peoples work environment are inhibitory to creativity. A typical symptom of this could, for example, be the reply "don't ask me, I only work here, I'm not paid to think" when posing questions. An over-inflated ego ("I know all the answers anyway") is equally inhibitory.

Thus organizations and individuals need to seek the stimuli for creativity they must also be on guard against that which holds creativity back. Inhibitors to creativity include:

- Fear factors &
- Screen factors.

These two factors can be broken down, each into four components.

Fear factors are those inhibitors that hold either an organization or an individual back from achieving aspects of creativity because they are frightened. So what are they frightened of?	
Change generally	In reality change is normal, however most people do not readily welcome it, nor actively seek it. Change is resisted. The status quo, stability and the retention of known certainty dominate. This does not allow for the incubation of creativity. Hanging on to the past is not a good basis for building a creative future.
Making mistakes	If organizations and hence individuals are worried about making mistakes, then they will never take risks and equally never do or think anything new.

| Looking foolish | This is often one of the largest barriers to creativity and one that is difficult to remove. None of us likes to appear foolish to others and the security of non-action avoids the risk of ridicule. However, the return is static non-creativity. |
| Non conformity | Anyone with teenage children will be familiar with this fear. The fear of not being the same as everyone else, being the odd one out. Being different and not coming up with the "expected" answer is the corn seed of creativity, and what innovative organizations should be actively seeking. |

Screen factors are those inhibitors that organizations and people hide behind and use as an excuse or justification for not being creative. So they hide behind:

| Time pressure | How many of us have felt a perverse sense of relief in having to work late or take on extra duties knowing full well that it's the perfect excuse for not redecorating the lounge! (I would be creative and I'm sure I am a really creative person, but unfortunately I'm too busy with day to day operational issues to take time out to think). How convenient! |
| Status | It is of course far easier to be a critic than a creator. We can all "red pen" someone else's work. The hard part is creating something in the first place. We are trained to be critical and judgmental in our approach rather than creative. Organizations tend to reinforce that rationale by both structure and status as embodied in organizational hierarchies. How often do we feel better about |

	ourselves if we are able to be critical of someone else or their work?
Structure	This links to the point above except the screen inhibitor is more specific to the organization. Organizations often do not structure themselves in a flexible and creative fashion. The top down approach is a powerful inhibitor of creativity. Organizational culture is not conducive to and supportive of new ideas or the non-conformist. In reverse this can also be the ideal excuse for the individual (I am creative but the organization prevents, limits, inhibits my natural flair). Again, how convenient!
Self	If the fear of non-conformity is a major inhibitor, perhaps the other is ourselves. We all have a great tendency to modesty and self-effacement! Self-defeating self-criticism is not a recipe for creativity. Again how easy to hide behind the "I'm not up to it" screen.

Are these factors real pressures, or are they simply a reflection of how we perceive situations and our view of the world? In the long run, it doesn't matter if they are subjective or objective, because, as seen under innovation, creativity is something that is positive and should be nurtured. Like innovation, creativity, in its fullest sense, involves both generating an idea and manifesting it (making something happen, although in business this may be labeled as problem solving).

Thus it would appear to be a good idea, if people could increase their creativity. How can this be done? Of course, creativity's other big enemy is stress, so it may be a good idea to take a break and go on holiday. However one of the first tasks in becoming more creative, is giving yourself permission to do things creatively. The second task is to overcome the aforementioned personal blocks. For some people, being creative involves trying not to be embarrassed by their ideas, for others it is a matter of being aware that things can be done in many different ways.

It is important to remember that creativity occurs (for most of us) in steps. The attitude "Sistine Chapel or Bust" is counter-productive, we are not all Einstein's, but someone wins the Nobel Prize anyway.

The steps to action are:

- Study books on creative thinking techniques and put them into practice. These include books by Edward DeBono and his ideas on brainstorming, provocation, creative & lateral thinking, six thinking hats, etc.
- Attend courses on creative thinking etc.
- Keep a daily journal and see what ideas can be developed. This follows a cycle of brainstorm, evaluate, harvest the useful ideas
- Indulge in relaxation activities and sport, to give your mind a rest and thus time to subconsciously digest information.
- Develop an interest in a variety of different things, preferably quite different from your normal sphere of work. This will give your brain a holiday from "chewing over" the same old stuff, and will open the doors to "cross-fertilization" of ideas.
- Don't work too hard. You need time away from a problem to be able to see it in perspective.
- Try to practice by doing everyday things in novel ways (it can be quite entertaining).
- Do not become overawed by huge problems. Anything can be achieved by breaking large problems down into their many component parts.
- Take one "bite" at a time and have the patience and willingness to work towards a creative outcome (rather than wait passively for miraculous enlightenment).

Creativity can come, but it must be an active process. A program to improve creativity may include several steps, including:

- Practice overcoming irrational inhibitions (if any). This may include your ego!
- Set a measurable goal, e.g. generate 10% more solutions next month, come up with a solution to "problem X" within two weeks, practice brainstorming with your group, find new way to relate to the children resulting in them wanting to spend 25% more time with me.
- Set up criteria to indicate whether you have reached your goal, e.g. time (deadline) criteria, or are the ideas novel (in that context), do the

ideas solve the problem or meet the challenge, can they be implemented within the appropriate time and budget.

- Surround yourself with people who love and respect you. They will encourage you. On the other hand, crossing an emotional desert without water is, in itself, a tasking proposition.
- Celebrate your progress. Life is a series of ever-harder exams. It is too easy to neglect that which you have achieved because you are overawed by the next step.
- Finally, act like a creative person. You will begin to think of yourself as a creative person and identify with your creative abilities. Thus you will find environments which support creative behavior.

Creativity is about not allowing your (perhaps too narrow, too modest or too self-effacing) beliefs to distort your perceptions of reality. A useful technique is to deliberately try to incorporate opposites. See things from the other person's point of view. Develop the attitude that what you do (as creative work) is important, even if others do not share your belief. After all, that is their problem, not yours, e.g. paint pictures, even if the result is horrible, it is primarily meant for you, not for a wide audience (remember that Van Gogh never managed to sell a painting whilst he was alive). Practice using affirmation and "re-framing" (seeing things from an unusual angle or in a different context) in order to de-program your self-critical habits. A sense of humor - especially black humor - helps immeasurably.

Summary
Creativity is an essential part of human existence. In everyday work situations, creativity is all to often quashed by bad management ("the bureaucratic mind"). The essential creativity in every person can be revived by conscious striving and mental exercises.

6. The Computer Revolution

Wages in the "First World" countries are high, whilst commodity prices are relatively cheap. This is because by using a computer each worker is now doing a job that it would have taken many men to do only 50 years ago. Conversely a small "personal" computer (PC) costs only about 10 - 15 man-days wages, so firms are able to keep costs low by investing in computers, rather than in expensive labor. Simultaneously unemployment is dropping because the computer industry is creating previously unknown business areas as well as opening previously unprofitable areas. These areas can be exploited especially by Small and Medium-sized Enterprises (SMEs) and, becoming more common, micro-business. Micro-businesses may be one or two people, who may have a normal job, but work a micro-business in their spare time.

Most people expect to pay a little more each year for services and things. Exactly the opposite is the case with computers. During the last decade hardware costs have dived, despite that PC memory (RAM), secondary memory (disk space) and processing speeds double each year. This is a bad situation for hardware producers but excellent for e-commerce business people. The recent developments in Object-Oriented Programming (OOP) make programs easier to understand, correct, modify & re-use, thus saving expensive programmer time. However the e-commerce business people must be able to understand the applicability and use of each type of program, and its programming language, in order not to make expensive mistakes.

Standing alone, a PC computer is just an advanced typewriter. By joining PCs in a network one operator can look in files on a different PC. To establish a network each computer needs to have a net card installed into the motherboard. The net card also has a cable plug to joint the computer to the network. Networks are of two types, LAN and WAN.

LANs (local access network) can be of two types, peer-to-peer, or client-server. Peer-to-peer is simply where the programs and utilities (printers, scanners etc) are shared between computers. Client server is where a specialized central computer with special software (a server) controls facilities. Individual computers (called workstations, clients or requesters) log on to the server and gain access to central facilities (e-mail, network printers, large databases, a central back up etc). This software is often very specialized (NT4, Novell or, for big networks, UNIX). LANs are characterized by the computers being physically connected by a special cable. These are either co-axial BNC ("thicknet"), or a type of telephone cable connected to a central hub (Ethernet or "thinnet"). These cables are connected to each computers net card, which in turn is plugged directly into the motherboard. Many LANs are a mixture of peer-to-peer and client-server.

WANs (wide access networks) connect computers in different parts of the world. The connection is usually by a telephone data line, although television and other types of cable networks are increasingly being used. Computers in one place are gathered in a LAN around the gateway, a modem (modulator-demodulator) controlled either by a specialized computer (a proxy server) or a router, and their data is received by a similar gateway on the other end, to be spread around the second LAN.

To illustrate this, think of a home PC. This may have a modem that can connect to PC to an ISP (Internet Service Provider). Once the modem has allowed the PC to log in, then the ISPs server will allow access to the Internet, which is a kind of public, super large WAN.

Summary
Cheap computers are raising labor efficiency and opening business areas that previously were too labor-intensive to be profitable. Thus IT areas are profitable grounds for entrepreneurs. The Internet is probably the most innovative environment yet created.

7. The IT industry

IT (Information Technology) refers to the collection of products and services that turn data into meaningful information. Sometimes the term ICT (Information & Communication Technology) is used, because telecommunication technology often overlaps with IT, and it can be difficult to tell the two apart.

The USA is the world leader in IT, representing around 35% of global spending on IT. IT has been a powerful source of employment. Approximately 20000 of the IT companies in the USA employ 50 or more persons and well over 10 million Americans earn their living by using IT (where 85% of these people do not work in the IT branch). IT has a compound long-term growth rate of 6.7% in the USA, compared to around 6% in the other G-8 countries. However the real importance of IT is in contributing to productivity growth; even in the years 2000 to 2002 US productivity growth was positive at between 2% and 5.2%. Simultaneously inflation has been held low by declining computer prices. The net effect has been that IT (roughly 7% of all US businesses) accounted for around 28% of overall US real economic growth between 1996 and 2000.

Spending on IT in the USA was almost 813 billion dollars in 2001, corresponding to about 3000 dollars per American.

Who uses IT? In 2002 the breakdown was as follows:

Who uses IT? Figures in % of all spending.	
Spending most:	
Financial services	6.64
Telecommunications	6.40
Banking	5.37
Spending least:	
Retail	1.63
Hospitality & Travel	1.55
Construction & Engineering	1.43

In comparison, the IT industry itself account for just over 5% of all spending on IT.

The future of IT can be reduced to one word; convergence. Convergence can be illustrated by looking at the breakthrough that came after analog voice, music, graphic and video formats were digitized, making all possible simultaneously, thus creating multimedia. Another example is Internet protocols, which is making worldwide knowledge sharing possible. Predictions of future convergence areas include mobile platforms and intelligent devices.

Whilst software applications and hardware construction are converging, the same is happening on the business side of the industry. In trying to predict the next wave, mergers and acquisitions (M&A) blur the traditional distinctions between infrastructure, applications and content providers. Furthermore smaller firms working on experimental unproven technologies may be competing to develop industry standards, and it is not unknown for several such firms to be bought by the same larger company, in order to assure the larger company that, whichever technology "wins", it has backed the winner.

Summary
The IT industry is small, but its importance lies in its "enabling" power for other industries. Using IT enables other industries to improve efficiency and, especially, retain productivity growth during times of recession.

8. Innovative enterprises.

New innovative enterprises, are often created by way of one of the following three possibilities:

- Classical start-up using capital provided by a 3rd party
- "Organic growth"; starting a small business (micro-business) "on the side" and see how it goes.
- Spin-off from a larger firm.

These three possibilities represent 3 general categories, with much variation within each category. For example the first "classical" method used to aim at an IPO (Initial Public Offering) on the stock exchange. Aiming for this is now rare.

Micro-businesses can be quite large if many people spend their spare time working in one, and this is achieving significance amongst community-based non-profit organizations.

Spin-offs can be created by a variety of ways, ranging from benevolent help from the mother organization, to the results of mass firings. Classically spin-offs emerge from university environments, and can grow to very large entities (e.g. the German optical firm Zeiss). Furthermore the 3 categories overlap, e.g. a university spin-off developing new technology may well be a candidate for 3rd party capital. This is common in e.g. the biotechnology branch.

One thing which all of the above have in common, is innovation.

The innovation "creed":

- Innovation is manageable and must be managed.
- Innovation is about finding new ways to deliver customer satisfaction.
- Innovation is about finding and building upon competitive advantage.
- Innovation is about rewriting the rules.
- Innovation is about strategy.
- Innovation is a process, not an isolated event.
- Innovation overturns the status quo and establishes a new vision.

Innovative ideas invariably come from individuals. However turning ideas into products is teamwork. Thus innovative enterprises often consist of teams with key individuals. The key individuals in this process are the so-called "product champion" and "business innovator". They may (or may not) be synonymous with the entrepreneur. The role of the entrepreneur is to link social need with invention, and without such entrepreneurial activity many good ideas never make it as innovations.

The product champion enthusiastically supports the innovation, especially during its critical phases. The latter, the manager with overall control of the project, is also highly committed to the innovation and plays a key role in welding the different phases together into one continuous innovation process. This manager coordinates design activity during basic development, prototype production, and manufacturing. It is his/her duty to ensure that the product is designed with easy manufacture in mind and, most importantly, to make sure that at all times the focus of design activity is on the satisfaction of user needs.

To start up you will need enormous enthusiasm and drive. Do you have a good idea? You need STRUCTURE and CONTENT:

Are you someone who "goes up" in your specialty? You'll need to be to have an idea no one else has had! Are you a "Nerd"? It's OK, Nerds are often fabulous experts in their field, but are Nerds equipped to survive in a sophisticated economic & business environment? Nerds have content, but little structure. One of the most famous, Thomas Eddison, went broke 4 times, and then only had marginal financial success. On the other hand, do you burn to market something? Anything?? What about the latest psycho-theory in HR written by a California guru who's just been on a TV talk show - yeah! That's got to sell well! Looks like you've got structure but little content. There are lots of one-man "management consultants" (or whatever name) around, and they stay 1-man firms! Structure and content complement each other. Partnerships where one delivers the content and the other the structure, are the simplest forms of Strategic Alliance. This involves trust, but deep friendship is not really needed. Indeed, don't expect a personal friendship afterwards. The "Manager" part of the team may well "go on" with the professional leadership after an IPO, and may well end up with more money. The "Nerd" may be resentful ("…he made millions out of my ideas … "), which will provoke the "Manager" ("…with my talent I could have picked up anybody, he'd still have nothing if it weren't for me...").

The recognition of the quite different roles of these two key people has become legendary in the field of innovation. One anecdote is that in my class "Innovation Management" at the IT University of Copenhagen, I introduce the fictitious company "Bullshitter & Nerd, Inc.". The simple fact is that most entrepreneurs are weak on the financial management side and this is especially the case for engineer entrepreneurs, indeed entrepreneurs from a "technical" background will find the Marketing/Sales challenges a very difficult area, whereas the entrepreneur must be the firm's best sales/marketing person. Therefore it is a good idea to team up with someone who can balance your capabilities (e.g. an engineer will need an MBA). In Apple, Jobs was the entrepreneur and Wozniack was the inventor, in HP, Hewlett was the engineer and Packard was the businessman. You can't do everything, so team up with someone with similar interests and different talents.

Do you personally have both structure and content? Lucky you. When such a person starts a firm they know and can do all jobs. As the firm expands more will be employed, most often through personal contacts, but still the "boss", despite informality (often-extreme informality) will still be theoretically able to do all jobs, s/he simply has to have employees because s/he has no time!

Choosing the right partner requires that you decide if you actually need one, and if, then decide if you actually need a partner, or if an employee will do. People have a very different attitude when they are owners or when they are employees. Also, while it is natural to choose a friend for a business partner, it seldom makes good business! A friend is emotionally involved, sensitive, understanding, shielding, protecting, supporting, whilst a business owner (partner) requires accurate information, straight answers, no surprises, tough decisions, immediate "bad news" and allegiance to the company, not the individual. Family intrusion can also be very difficult.

How to choose a partner:

- Don't choose a loner, s/he must be able to work with people.
- Ensure s/he has a winning track record, don't tie up with a loser.
- Partner with an experienced entrepreneur. Half the business failures are due to incompetent management.
- Assure appropriate commitment level. Load sharing must be agreed upon, then delivered on.
- Check references on the prospective partner.
- From the start, build a clear method of exit for a partner
- Deal with any "life partner" problem from the very start.

Turning an idea or invention into profit demands an organization. Flexibility is a key quality in an innovative organization, thus flat hierarchical pyramids which push decision-making downwards are typical characteristics of the innovative enterprise. They have an entrepreneurial and matrix type management structure, which preserves an efficient monitoring system and discipline essential in any organization. Indeed innovative enterprises tend to have fluid, organic structures rather than rigid mechanistic ones. This encourages decision-making, problem solving and creative thinking with policies and guidelines being used, rather than rules, and this team creativity in turn promotes the improvement of existing products, systems and services. To create team creativity within an organization needs real commitment from the top. Leaders who encourage creativity have some distinct characteristics:

- A willingness to accept risks.
- An ability to work with half-baked ideas.
- A willingness to bend the rules.
- An ability to respond quickly.
- Personal enthusiasm

All members involved in the activities of an organization can participate in the innovation process, with people who have hands-on experience of the various processes being in a good position to suggest incremental improvements. A feeling of belonging to, and being part of, the enterprise helps to motivate employees and fosters team creativity. Innovation is more than having new ideas: it includes the process of successfully introducing them or making things happen in a new way. It turns ideas into useful, practicable and commercial products or services.

Summary
Technological start-ups need two key figures, the technologist who develops the product, and the manager who sells the idea and looks after the business. Start-ups and other innovative enterprises are characterized by a flat structure, which promotes the individuals creativity.

9. The psychological wringer.

Founding a start-up is, for the entrepreneur, the beginning of a passage through a psychological mill, where the demand for mental agility and flexibility will simply grind that person down. No one comes through the process unchanged. This calls for mental resilience and aptitude, the right attitude and unbreakable will power. Be clear about that this is what you want to do for the next several years. The entrepreneur will have to be able to focus completely on one area in one moment, then be able to switch and make the right decision in another area a moment later. Experience shows that actually few possess these qualities, and thus training and delegation become important. Conversely "serial entrepreneurship" is habit-forming. Seasoned entrepreneurs get used to the freedom and may find it difficult to go back to a normal job, as they can make very bad employees. Starting up involves:

* Hard work
* Lots of anxiety and frustration
* High failure rate (over 99.9%)

Marco Polo, the "first" entrepreneur, was financed by venture capitalists, he paid 22.5% interest on the money and the venture capitalist retained 75% of the profits. Some trends include that 42,000 businesses fail each year, but about 2 million new companies are being formed every year. The two big new influences are immigrants & women, but 50% of college students consider an entrepreneurial career.

As an example of mental stress one can look at the chain of ideas typical of a start-up, in order to illustrate the flexibility involved.

1. Idea phase. Collegial discussion with like-minded people.
2. Development phase. Getting deep into the technicalities.
3. Preparing the business plan. A mountain of paper work and business research.
4. Selling the idea to a circle of investors.
5. Roll out and concentrate on selling the product to end-users.
6. More marketing, intensive selling, whilst modifying the product according to customer demands.
7. Exit, sell your "baby", or at least relinquish majority control.

It is quite obvious that each one of these six stages demands quite a different mind-set, and that is a huge wrench to go from one stage to the next. And if that wasn't bad enough, it is quite obvious that what your firm needs to start-up successfully, and what your firm needs to keep going successfully, are two completely different things. For example let us assume that the initial phases have been successfully completed, followed by more expansion, perhaps adding a financial/wage section. The bank and potential investors are visiting, where is the boss' business suit? What does the boss know about "doing the books"? ledgers? loans? business intelligence? At this point 2 things can happen:

- The boss continues as sole boss, chaos everywhere, boss has physical/mental breakdown, firm fails.
- The boss hires competent specialists, a "Board" and becomes division head (typically "Development" where an informal atmosphere promotes new products), firm succeeds.

The conclusion of the above is find out what you want, before you start. This could be:

- A personal SME that will provide you with interest & income for 30 years (i.e. a large part of a small cake).
- A mega-success involving hard fights until you are the worlds biggest (i.e. a small part of a large cake).
- A project challenge, which you can sell for a million dollars after 3 years (i.e. a vehicle for your subsequent efforts or life style).

This choice will have a profound impact on your strategy, right down to your choice of legal entity for your firm, Ltd, PLC etc (where PLC here stands for Public Limited Company).

It is important to realize that firms have Life Cycles - just as its products have Life Cycles (Product Life Cycle - PLC - not the be confused with Public Limited Company). These indeed are very similar, apart from that a cycle for a product will typically be five years and that for a firm, up to thirty years.

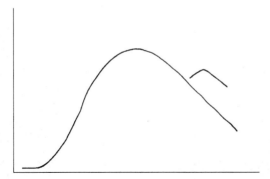

The above figure represents sales or value versus time during an idealized life cycle, for either a company or a product. The small "hump" represents the introduction of a rejuvenating factor. In a company this could be a new manager. In a PLC it could be a new sales channel, e.g. airline tickets being offered over the Internet.

The different kinds of leadership a firm gets as it progresses through its Life Cycle are sketched out below (for more details see, Mellor, The Web Managers Handbook, 2003).

1. The Startup Stage - Adventurer Managers.
2. The Hockey-stick Stage - Warrior Managers.
3. The Professional Stage - Hunter Managers.
4. Mature and Consolidating Stage - Farmer Managers.
5. The Declining Stage Politician Managers.
6. The Sustaining Stage - Turnaround (Visionary) Managers.

It is very important to find out which type of manager that you, as entrepreneur, are, because it clearly has to match with the developmental stage (i.e. Adventurer or Warrior in a new start-up). It is also equally important to note that your temperament will not fit all stages, and to insist on retaining control throughout the life cycle will indubitably harm your enterprise.

Summary
Few are prepared for the enormous mental strain involved in starting a new firm. Being open, and realizing that you are not the best person to control your firm, can partially compensate for this. This is useful in selecting the type of help needed, and in selecting an exit strategy.

10. The investor chain.

Often a start up will go to a network or similar organization in order to get contacts. Some of these organizations can be government funded. Typing "business angel" or "venture capital" into a search engine will normally result in a series of hits. In the USA, UK & Scandinavia help can be found via Connect, which is a non-profit making organization helping those looking to attract investors. Connect will give help and sparring in connection with the business plan. They can give help independently of whether investment capital is the goal, or if the organic growth path to an SME or micro-business, is the chosen way.

Investors can come in several shades. There is government help, incubators, business angels and venture capitalists. Their aims, their willingness to take risks, and the amounts they invest, are all different. Especially government-sponsored schemes change often. Getting into this pipeline is important. Once an investment has been made, the investor and the start-up have a common goal, selling the investment further down the stream to the next, bigger, investor.

For an entrepreneur with an idea and who approaches a government-supported innovation environment (incubator etc.) , the chain may look like this:

Step	Name	Content
1	Making the idea more concrete.	Discussion, including: • Networking generally or at the university. • Conferences. • Arrangements (lectures etc). • Partners and friends.
2	First contact with an innovation environment.	By means of web-site, or personally. • Presenting the idea. • Sending material for evaluation. • Feedback with meeting (especially if positive).
3	Screening	• Delivery of supplementary material. • Meeting. • Internal discussion in the innovation environment. • Follow-up with "go/no-go".

4	Research Here, at the latest, a company of some type will have to be established, assuming that none existed previously.	• Thorough analysis of the process. • Detailed analysis. • Business Plan. • Budget/Financial plan. • IPR (Intellectual Property Rights) and other rights. • Patentability check. • Technical analysis. • Market analysis. • A Project Team is assembled, including representatives of the innovation environment.
5	Contract	• First round of contract negotiations. • Presentation of the project. • Nomination for pre-seed capital. • Contract negotiations finish, how big a share the innovation environment gets of the company, in return for how much money. • First investment. Investments are mostly paid out in rates, dependent on milestones.
6	Pre-project	• Physical framework - offices etc. • Network. • Consulting and other advice (e.g. book-keeping). • Development of prototype. • Patent strategy. • Sales & marketing. • Business development. • Hiring co-workers. • Management team (normally including participation of members of the innovation environment). • Board of Directors (professionals from various relevant branches).
7	Exit	Passing the project on to further investors. • Making a brochure. • Making contact with investors. • Presentation of project. • Negotiations.

Very few ideas get accepted for funding. Business plan competitions show an acceptance rate of well under 1%.

	Ideas	Business Plans	Seed Funding
Biotech (USA)	1000	100	56
IT (EU)	400	25	12
High Tech (EU)	182	20	5

The reasons why the business plans were rejected is broken down as follows:

Reason for rejection	Number
Weak management team	52
Not market driven	38
Timeframe too long	31
Financial commitment too large	25
Lack of patentability	15
Inadequate technical expertise	12
Other (various)	17

The point that most start-ups have a weak management team is driven home by the way high-tech SMEs regard themselves, 91% are confident in their technical ability, but only 27% are confident that they get their ideas to the market in an acceptable time frame. This again underlines the point:

- The major factor in obtaining investment is a strong management and sales team, combined with a Board of Directors which inspires confidence

When an investor is looking an investment object, s/he knows that a strong sales team can sell anything, so there will always be some return on investment. However even a brilliant technical idea, without sales, will never return the investment, and the invested money goes down the drain. Fortunately innovation environments (incubators etc) and many Business Angels will be able to suggest members of the Board of Directors.

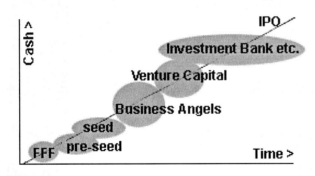

This figure shows a (theoretical) investment chain for a start-up. In times of boom the players will move down the curve towards the origin. In times of recession, the players will move to the upper right, leaving large "holes" around the origin. In times of recession BAs and VCs may furthermore get together to merge "their" companies (M&A, Mergers and Acquisitions) in order both to streamline their portfolios and to optimize benefits of scale within individual holdings.

Initial investment comes from the entrepreneurs' savings and those people around him/her. This stage is called FFF, which stands for Friends, Family and Fools. Seed capital (and pre-seed capital) often comes from public sources, as described for innovation environments. Many innovation environments will have their own incubators (science park etc.) which can house the new company. Science Parks offer a complete infrastructure, which a small start-up may otherwise not be able to afford, plus the additional benefit of synergy between small firms.

A typical innovation environment may invest up to one million dollars each year in between five and (max.) ten start-ups. The innovation environments "customers" are often BAs, their customers, in turn, may be Venture Capitalists, and theirs, as proof of concept is established and risk diminished, are, in turn, investment banks or the investment branch of a regular bank. They get their Return on Investment (ROI) from members of the public, either by selling products to the public, selling the company to a larger firm (takeover) or selling stock on the stock exchange after an IPO (Initial Public Offering).

Summary
Investment occurs in several stages. The main reason for lack of
investment is weak management. This often poses a dilemma for the
entrepreneur, who may not be able to pay for professional help. Publicly
funded innovation environments may be able to help.

11. Types of investment.

The type and extent of investment will vary from start-up to start-up. This is a consequence of different types of product. Normally one start-up has only one product. One of the major factors is TTM (Time To Market).

Of the many patents granted each year, only an extreme minority ever gets used commercially. Of these few, the vast majority represents incremental innovation, where the new product can be applied almost immediately (i.e. TTM is short).

Clearly if you are borrowing a business concept from another country (sometimes called "creative imitation"), or simply importing something not found locally (e.g. through buyusa.com), then the application can be called close-to-use. Here the proof of concept has already been clearly established, TTM is very short and no significant investments in research & development are needed (but perhaps significant investments in marketing).

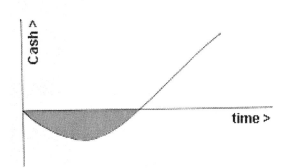

The above figure shows cash flow for a start-up. Clearly at the start of operations, products are not being sold. They may not be ready, or may need a market breakthrough. Thus the gray area represents the investment needed. For a new service with a short TTM, the "rule of thumb" is that the first customer buys within 3-6 months of starting, and the plus/minus point ("break-even", where the curve again passes through the X axis), is reached after 18-24 months. For this type of operation a Business Angel may be useful, but otherwise the entrepreneur may choose to approach a bank for a regular loan. Note that break-even point is not the same as the point of completed repayments, the time needed to repay investments will stretch much further to the right.

For large projects, like developing new hardware (or new medicines), the gray area may stretch over five years or more, and represent an investment of many tens of millions of dollars. Typically financing for such projects will involve seeking funding from a BA (initially), and then Venture Capital. After many such financing rounds the original entrepreneur may only own 10% of the company.

Investors, both BAs and VCs, can often be found using investor relations firms. Examples are:

Some investor relations firms	
Compass Point Group	www.compasspointgroup.com
FitzGerald Communications	www.fitzgerald.com
Morgen-Walke Associates	www.morgen-walke.com
Pondel/Wilkinson Group	www.pondel.com

Business angels (BAs) are a relatively new phenomenon. They are often entrepreneurs who have started up a company and exited with an excess of cash. They are ready to invest this surplus in new start-ups. Typically a BA will invest around 250 000 dollars for a variable percentage of stock. The BAs contribution, however, is even more, since the BA wants to be involved in running the start-up, so the start-up gets hands-on help. The BAs help, experience and network of contacts is often of immeasurable help, and the BA may take a nominal salary for such work. Thus the BA may take 25% of the company (this is, of course, purely a matter of negotiation) for 250000 dollars. This implies a valuation of one million dollars for the company - quite obviously this is most often an overvaluation! However the task the BA has taken on, either alone or in syndication with other BAs, is to personally work towards increasing the companies' value to e.g. 4 million within one or two years. At this time his/her share will have a value of one million dollars. Obviously the harder the BA works, the higher the potential return. This is often called "active investment".

Venture Capital is an older concept than Business Angel. The classical Venture Capital companies came into being in the 1980s (whereas BA is a concept beginning typically in 2000 or 2001). Individuals who are VCs are becoming rare. A typical setup will be a holding company that will set up a fund with a fixed lifetime. Investors are invited and, when the fund has reached a certain size, investment objects will be found. Typically the fund closes to investors when a certain volume has been reached, and the fund has a limited lifetime (typically ten years with the option of a two year extension), after which it is dissolved and the proceeds repaid to the investors. Venture capital requires less risk than earlier forms of investment. However such investors are very professional, and at this point the entrepreneur has probably less than 50% of the company. Thus failure to meet milestones will often result in closing the investment. Indeed investments can be closed for other, quite external, reasons, including where the entrepreneur has performed well. This, of course, leaves the entrepreneur empty-handed, and reasoning such as "if you close the company now, you will lose all your investment up to now" will hardly work. VC investments are much more passive than BA investments, however they will often contribute with salaried directors or members of an advisory board.

The size of the investment from a VC fund is, however, typically larger than earlier forms of investment, starting perhaps at one million dollars. Larger sums, perhaps over 2 million dollars, will often require that VC societies syndicate together.

One thing that is absolutely necessary when attracting investments from both BA and VC sources alike is that the formal demands placed on the company increase enormously. When attracting finance from an innovation environment, the company may be so small and new that few formal demands can be made. In the subsequent investment phases, this is quite different. The major processes are:

Non Disclosure Agreement.
Letter of Intent (or Term Sheet).
Due Diligence.

Due diligence is defined as: "*An examination of the books and records of a company and interviews with officers, partners etc., to confirm information about the company's business as well as legal and accounting affairs*".

The preliminary due diligence may take the form of a discussion about the business plan, interviews with the management, inviting comments from external analysts, potential customers, competitors, former workers and previous employers. This is then followed by an independent accountant's verification of the historical data. Finally lawyers will move in to verify everything about the legal framework the company exists in, including partner contracts to date, verification of patent, immaterial, and other rights assigned to the company, contracts with employees (especially incitement schemes like shares, options and warrants).

Options and warrants.

Shares ("stock") in a company costs money. How much money is determined by supply and demand. Options means buying the possibility of buying a share to an agreed price in the future. If an option is bought to buy a share to ten dollars in two years time, and the share price has risen to twenty dollars, then this is good business. Conversely the option may stipulate that the acquired share, if bought, cannot be resold within a stipulated time. This is especially relevant to employee options, where a sudden release of shares onto the market may well defeat the point of the exercise. Obviously if the share price has gone down to less that ten dollars, then the option will scarcely be used. Employees who have acquired a part of their salary as options will be disappointed.

Shares and options are part of the financial base that already exists, That is, a company having 10000 shares at 10 dollars each has, in principal, 100000 dollars of capital. Owning one of these gives the owner 0.001% of control. Warrants are different, because a warrant signifies the right to buy new shares, which do not exist at the time of signing. That is, the company acquires new capital with less dilution of the old capital.

A company having 10000 shares at 10 dollars each has, in principal, 100000 dollars of capital. If an employee has 1000 dollars in warrants, and decides to use the warrants (let us assume the stock price is unchanged), then the company will afterwards have 10100 shares, giving a total of 101000 dollars in share capital. So the company is relatively better off, whilst the previous shareholders have decreased relatively little, from 100% to 99.1% control.

Over and above the formal points, due diligence is meant to examine:

- What is the business model?
- What technology and know-how exists in the company?
- What is the product or service?
- Where is the competitive advantage?
- Are the material and immaterial rights secured?
- Are there any alliances?
- What is the relevant market, is it a growth market?
- What is the strategy with respect to customer segment, market segment and marketing generally?
- Need for financing and source of financing?

- Are the key workers there and can they be retained?
- What are the strengths and weaknesses of the management?
- How much expertise is needed where?

Due diligence should not probe into the entrepreneurs personal background and police record, but often does. Thus entrepreneurs with e.g. a history of serial bank robbery may prefer to come clean at a relatively early stage in negotiations.

Summary
Investments from Business Angels and Venture Capitalists are quite different. Investments from Business Angels are smaller and more active, in that the Business Angel works more closely with the firm than Venture Capital societies do. However both demand a thorough examination of the company set-up.

12. Setting up the company.

Doing business is not the same as having a company. Individual people may register themselves for tax and commence doing business. In the UK this goes under the name "sole trading" and in the USA it is called "general trading". People trading as a sole trader or general trader should realize that the person and the business are treated as one entity. This means that if there are any problems with the business, then the individual is personally liable for any debts the business incurs. This can put your house and any personal assets you might have at risk.

Sole traders can also enter into partnerships. In the USA and the UK profits from the partnership go to the individuals involved, who then pay income tax. However, the individuals are still personally liable if things go wrong. There are two exceptions to this rule: In Scotland it is possible that a partnership is taxed separately (although the partners still have liability). Also in the USA there is a widely-used construction called Limited Liability Company (LLC), where partners are still taxed as individuals, but their liability is limited.

Founding a Limited Company is a logical step for people wanting to do business and who are:

- Currently self-employed
- Working as a contractor
- Consultant
- In a business partnership
- Thinking of starting a business.

The advantages of a limited company include:

- If you have a limited company you are limiting your personal liabilities.
- A Limited Company is a legal entity in its own right. The owner is not personally liable for the company's debts, as long as the firm has traded legally (or if the owner has not given personal guarantees regarding contracts or suppliers etc.) If things go wrong, then the creditors are paid out of the company's assets not from the owners' own personal assets.

- Once you have chosen and registered your company name no other company can use the same name, unlike business, where names can be duplicated.
- Investors like BAs and VCs can buy parts of the firm (as shares, options, warrants etc) in return for money. They will never invest in a sole trader or anything else other than a firm.
- Getting a bank loan is much easier.

In the USA companies can be founded with the abbreviations Inc., Co., or Ltd (not to be confused with the British Ltd.). Companies are registered in the state they originate from, and not on a federal level. Thus the rules about how to set them up, how much capital is required, which licenses are needed, etc., vary from state to state, and thus can not be elaborated here.

In the England and Wales companies are assumed to be private companies, unless otherwise stated. Private companies are called "Limited" or "Ltd", and these terms are not interchangeable. Private companies must issue at least one share of minimum value one GB pound. Public companies must have an issued share capital of at least 50 000 GB pounds, where at least one-quarter has been paid-up. Public Limited Companies may use the abbreviation "PLC" (not to be confused with Product Life Cycle).

Setting up companies is a job for experts. Further details can be found at the web sites of the many companies who specialize in formations, e.g. uk-business-formations.co.uk, or Jordans.

However before setting up a company, it may be useful to consider groups of companies. The principle of have a Holding Company has become very popular. If a holding is an attractive construction, then it should be created first, and then the holding creates subsidiaries. Creating a holding later, when the holding has to buy an already-existing company, will result in a disadvantageous tax situation. In principle an entrepreneur can create a holding (such companies are entitled to use the word "holdings" in their name, although this is not obligatory), and use that to create subsidiaries for each start-up project. One holding can have many subsidiaries. Similarly, one subsidiary may be owned by several companies, of which none, some, or all, can be holdings. The advantage of holdings is that if one company fails, then the others will not be affected. There are also tax advantages insomuch as profits can be transferred from subsidiaries to holdings at reduced tax rates. However tax planning with groups of companies needs professional advice and great care.

It should be underlined that, especially when setting up a UK company, shares represent cash. Including collateral in capital is very rare. This is in contrast to several EU countries, where an accountant signs that the new company has the required amount of capital (25 000 Euros for a GmbH, 18 000 Euros for an ApS etc.), which, in turn, can be a mixture of cash and collateral. Collateral may include valuable domain names, patent rights, even a PC etc.

However, even when patents cannot contribute to share capital, they can be a powerful contribution to the evaluation of a company's value. Program source code is protected by copyright (even when easy to change) however many fail to patent a programs use, for example it may be possible to patent making GUIs, using your code as an example. Trade marks, business methods and other protectable aspects (domain names etc) may further add value. Patent law changes often, so it is always advisable to consult an expert, even when you may not be sure that you have anything to protect.

Summary
Creating a limited company is an essential step towards expansion. This enables the entrepreneur to attract financing whilst limiting personal liability. Incorporation exists in several forms, each with advantages and disadvantages, especially with regard to tax.

13. The strategic business proposition.

For a business to be successful it has to have a narrow in-depth focus. This will enable the entrepreneur to plan what amounts of money and effort is needed. Thus the business proposition needs to define how attractive the proposed market is, if the entrepreneur is capable of capturing that market, and what targets to strive for. Research and experience shows that firms with a strategy perform better, firms without a strategy are more likely to fail, however that having a strategy is no guarantee of success. The primary strategic questions are; where are we now? Where do we want to go? And how will we get there?

Porter
The ability of a firm to create and sustain profits will depend on how many other firms are operating in the same market niche, how easy it is for other firms to invade that territory, and on the bargaining power of suppliers and buyers. Michael Porter formalized this intuition about determinants of "industry attractiveness" into what he called the 5-forces framework.

Rivalry amongst sellers already in the marketplace depends on factors such as the number of firms in the industry, their relative size and how hard they fight each other for market share. If only one firm exists, then a monopoly exists. If two or more firms inhabit that market, then rivalry exists which will constrain the ability of firms to set prices and generate profits. Higher degrees of rivalry (more firms) can make markets unattractive. Potential competition refers to that inhabiting a market successfully may mean the generation of above-normal profits. This is likely to attract potential competitors, and if new entry takes place, then prices and profits are likely to fall. However, if there are "barriers to entry", for example patent rights, then profits will be easier to sustain.

Alternative products or services refer to the ability of substitutes to reduce profits. For example manufacturers of glass bottles would make much more money if there were no plastic bottles or cans.

Customers' purchasing power refers to the ability of buyers to negotiate about purchase price. Clearly if buyers are powerful, then they may squeeze prices and profits. Similarly suppliers' position in the market refers to the ability of suppliers to negotiate prices, or even, if there are very few suppliers, terminate supply.

Industries are likely to be unattractive if they consist of many rivals, easy entry, several close substitutes, powerful buyers and suppliers. Thus by using a Porter analysis the entrepreneur can assess the market and avoid unattractive markets.

Porters original 5 force model has been modified by adding a sixth: Interest groups (Greenpeace etc), which have an influence if a product is offensive to environmental, women's, etc pressure groups. If industry attractiveness is good to excellent, then build and invest. If it is medium, then protect and milk, but if poor, then exit and sell.

Strategic Group Mapping.
After completing a preliminary Porter-type analysis, more details are obtained using strategic group mapping. This also enables the entrepreneur to see what are the Critical Success Factors (CSFs).

Step 1: Identify competitive characteristics that differentiate firms in an industry. This also give good clues to what the CSFs are. These may be:

- Price/quality
- Geographic coverage
- Degree of vertical integration
- Product line breadth
- Use of distribution channels
- Degree of service

Step 2: Plot the competitors on graph using pairs of differentiating characteristics as axes.
Step 3: Assign firms that fall in about the same strategy space to the same strategic group.

Step 4: Draw circles around each strategic group, making the circles proportional to the size of the group's market share. Then it is possible to rate firm and rivals on a scale of 1 to 10.

Then weight the CSFs by importance, multiply rate by weight/weighted rate, sum the weighted rates and evaluate where you stand competitively. At this stage data collection may be important, e.g. collect competitor business information from reputable sources, e.g. yahoo and Companies House, do customer surveys on-line, do they visit the competition? Some also subscribe to competitor's mailing lists to find out what they think is new. Whatever solution appears, never copy your competitors. If you take from others you will never be first! However it is legitimate to ask how other companies have solved similar problems.

SWOT

Having assessed the attractiveness of the proposed market and identified competitors and CSFs, the next task is to see if the proposed company can actually inhabit that market. This is called company situation analysis. The key issues include; cost competitiveness, competitive position, what problems need to be addressed, market share and competitive advantage. These can be addressed using a SWOT analysis. SWOT stands for Strengths, Weaknesses, Opportunities and Threats. SWOT analyses often consist of a matrix:

	Positive	**Negative**
Internal	Strengths	Weaknesses
External	Opportunities	Threats

A SWOT analysis enables "killer assumptions" to be identified in time. These could be manifested under Weaknesses or Threats. Furthermore it should be useful in locating a firms core competencies, something that a company does better than the competition. Examples could be:

- Know-how
- Quality control
- Service capability
- Product design
- Marketing skills
- Quality of management

One of the subjects covered should be cost position relative to competitors, but raw materials supply, logistics, distribution etc., may enter the equation. Correcting a cost disadvantage may entail; tightening the budget, increasing productivity (equipment and employees), eliminating cost-producing activities, re-locating high cost activities geographically, redesign the product etc.

The beauty of SWOT analyses is that they can be applied almost everywhere. Individual products can be subjected to SWOT, as can competing firms, potential retailers etc. In any situation it can be used to determine if strengths heavily outweigh weaknesses, where the competitive advantage is, and are there any weak spots in the present strategy.

Mission Statement

The tasks of strategic management normally include:

- Defining business and mission.
- Establish objectives.
- Craft a strategy.
- Implement the strategy.
- Evaluate, review, and make adjustments.

The first task, developing a mission, needs a vision about where the company is headed over the next 5 years. This will inject it with a sense of purpose, provide long-term direction and give the organization an identity. Thus it is a good idea to establish a written mission statement. A good mission statement implies where the organization is, where it wants to go and in what market. An example of a Mission Statement is:

"Our mission is to expand our worldwide leadership in the spice, seasoning, and flavoring markets." (McCormick and Company)

Backing up the mission statement should be a program that establishes objectives. Without measurable objectives, a mission statement is just hot air. Objectives should be measurable, difficult, but doable, and should have a time frame. Examples could be:

- Achieve a 20% return on equity within 3 years.
- Achieve a net sales growth rate of 10% per year.
- Pay out 25% to 35% of net income in dividends per year.

- Within 5 years, achieve the largest market share in the industry.

Summary
An analysis according to "Porter Five Forces" is a preliminary study showing if a market is at all attractive. Strategic Group Mapping adds flesh to such analyses. SWOT matrices help analyze the ability of an organization to actually inhabit the market niche, whilst a Mission Statement gives an organization a sense of purpose.

14. Marketing plan.

The marketing plan explains in detail how the company's products will be sold. This is very important, even for companies with a long TTM. This is because a long TTM means very large investments, so investors need to know how their money will be returned. Companies with a short TTM will need an extremely detailed marketing plan. This includes specifying exactly who does what and when. For booksellers advertising is most important before Christmas, for travel agents, January and February and so forth. How will customers be reached? What media will be used? What does this cost? Who will take orders? By specifying that here, the ground is being laid for another important part of the business plan, the budget. However, despite going into the smallest detail, there must still be space for chance management.

Chance management.

Chance management (or opportunity management) starts by stating that it is wrong to let strategy get funneled into a fixed lane where it is difficult to change. Don't put all your eggs in one basket. Chance management stresses that, upon completing the next step, there should be a larger number of opportunities open than there were before taking that step.

This is needed because the development of many new products and services is customer-led, an intrinsically unknowable factor. There have been many observations that successful companies, and individuals, have a bias towards action, doing short experiments to feel out new technologies or markets and then quickly revising their plans and goals based on what they learn. They admit in advance they don't know all the answers and expect to be surprised. Similarly they avoid an emotional or ego fixation on their first plans or prototypes.

The customer is always your first and most important marketing challenge. Listen! Try to see the customers problems and needs from his/her point of view. Restate the problem and the customers needs in his/her terms and iterate until a consensus is reached. Ask not only what his/her problems are, but also what special methods or tools s/he is presently using to solve them. Studies of the sources of innovation in the electronics industry have concluded that more than 70% of the product innovations came from the users, who initially can't find the tools or equipment they need on the market and are forced to develop them themselves. Most companies ignore this process and consequently miss many good, easy opportunities for new products or product enhancements. Remember that the real objective is higher profits. Raising the selling price by adding value, or re-targeting the market, can be an alternative or supplement to cutting costs.

Sample Marketing Plan.

Title: Marketing Plan For Allyourwishes Technology Ltd.

1. 0 Executive Summary
Allyourwishes Technology Ltd will change its focus to differentiate itself from box pushers and improve the business by filling the real need of small business and high-end home office for reliable information technology including hardware, software, and all related services.

1.1 Vision
AYWT Ltd is built on the assumption that the management of information technology for business is like legal advice, accounting, graphic arts, and other bodies of knowledge, in that it is not inherently a do-it-yourself prospect. Smart business people who aren't computer hobbyists need to find quality vendors of reliable hardware, software, service, and support. They need to use those quality vendors like they use their other professional service suppliers, as a trusted ally.

AYWT Ltd is such a vendor. It serves its clients as a trusted ally, providing them with the loyalty of a business partner and the economics of an outside vendor. We make sure that our clients have what they need to run their business as well as possible, with the maximum efficiency and reliability. Many of our information applications are mission critical, so we give our clients the assurance they need that we will be there when they need us.

1.2 Objectives.
1.2.1. Increase sales by 20%
1.2.2. Increase gross margin to more than 25%.
1.2.3. Increase our non-hardware sales to 65% of the total.

2.0 Target Markets.
AYWT Ltd focuses on local markets, small business, with special focus on the high-end home office and the 5-20-unit small business office.

2.1 Market Definition and Segmentation.
We have broken our markets into groups according to standard

classifications used by market information companies: home offices and small business. We don't really need to provide exact definitions of each of these market segments, at least not for the purposes of making our marketing decisions. We know our home office customers tend to be heavy users, wanting high-end systems, people who like computing and computers. The low-end home office people buy elsewhere. We also know that our small business customers tend to be much less proficient on computers, much more likely to need and want hands-on support, and much more likely to pay for it.

2.2 Target Market Segment Strategy.
We cannot survive just waiting for anybody to walk in with business. Instead, we must get better at focusing on the specific market segments whose needs match our offerings. Focus on target segments is the key to our future. Therefore, we need to focus our message and our offerings. We need to polish the promise, make sure that our target segments hear the promise, and then make sure that we fulfil the promise.

2.3 Home Office.
The home offices in Ourtown are an important growing market segment. Nationally, there are approximately 30 million home offices, and the number is growing at 10% per year. Our estimate in this plan for the home offices in our market service area is based on an analysis published four months ago in the local newspaper. Home Offices (HOs) include several types. The most important, for our plan, are the home offices that are the only offices of real businesses, in which people make their complete living. These are likely to be professional services such as graphic artists, writers, and consultants, also some accountants and the occasional lawyer, doctor, or dentist. There are also home offices for part-time use, such as for people who are employed during the day but work at home at night, or for people who work at home to provide themselves with a part-time income, or people who maintain home offices because of their hobbies. Of these different types, we focus on the home office involved in somebody's full-time income. These are the professionals and entrepreneurs who work from their homes. In this plan we refer to them as HOs.

2.3.1 Needs and Requirements.
Our target HOs are on average as dependent on reliable information technology as any other businesses. They care more about reliable service and confidence than about the rock-bottom lowest price. They don't want to rely solely on their own expertise, so they choose instead to deal with us with our promise of service and support when needed. Our standard

HOs will be one-system installations, no networks, much more powerful systems than the average small business. Fax modems, voicemail, and good printers are likely. They tend to be interested in DTP, accounting, and administration software as well as their job-specific software needs. It's important that we realize we won't be selling to the price-oriented HO buyers. We'll be able to offer an attractive proposition to the service-oriented and security-oriented buyers only.

2.3.2 Distribution Channels.
Unfortunately our HO target buyers may not expect to buy with us. Many of them turn immediately to the superstores (office equipment, office supplies, and electronics) and mail order to look for the best price, without realizing that there is a better option for them at only a little bit more.

2.3.3 Competitive Forces.
Our focus group sessions indicated that our target HOs think about price but they would buy on quality service if the offering were properly presented. They think about price because that's all they ever see. We have very good indications that may would much rather pay 10-20% more for a relationship with a long-term vendor providing back-up and quality service and support; they end up in the box-pusher channels because they aren't aware of the alternatives. Availability is also very important. The HO buyers tend to want immediate solutions to problems. They hop into a car and seek a product that same instant.

2.3.4 Communications.
One of the best places to reach the target HO is the local newspaper. Unfortunately, that medium is saturated with pure-price-only messages, and we'll have to make sure that our message is excellently stated. Radio is potentially a good opportunity. Our HO target buyers listen to local news, talk shows, and sports. Seminars are a tough sell. The target HO buyer rarely has time for seminars. They think most seminars are thinly disguised sales pitches.

2.3.5 Keys to Success.
The main key to success with HO buyers, we believe, is making the business proposition clear. Many potential buyers would much prefer our offering to the box-only offerings of the chain stores and mail order sources, if only they knew the trade-off. Word of mouth is critical in this segment. We will have to make sure that once we gain a customer, we never lose them. We must always remember to sell the company, not the product. They have to understand they are taking on a relationship with

AYWT Ltd, not just buying boxes. Boxes they can get cheaper elsewhere.

2.4 Target Market: Small Business.
Small business in our market includes virtually any business with a retail, office, professional, or industrial location outside of someone's home, and fewer than 30 employees. We estimate 45,000 such businesses in our market area. The 30-employee cutoff is arbitrary. We find that the larger companies turn to other vendors, but we can sell to departments in larger companies, and we shouldn't be giving up leads when we get them.

2.4.1 Needs and Requirements.
Our target SBs are very dependent on reliable information technology. They use the computers for a complete range of functions beginning with the core administration information such as accounting, shipping, and inventory. They also use them for communications within the business and outside of the business, and for personal productivity. They are not, however, large enough to have dedicated computer personnel such as the MIS departments in large businesses. Ideally, they come to us for a long-term alliance, looking to us for reliable service and support to substitute for their in-house people. These are not businesses that want to shop for rock-bottom price through chain stores or mail order. They want to be sure they have reliable providers of expertise. Our standard SBs will be 5-20 unit installations, critically dependent on local-area networks. Back up, training, installation, and ongoing support are very important. We can virtually count on them needing database and administrative software as the core of their systems.

2.4.2 Distribution Channels.
The SB buyers are accustomed to buying from vendors who visit their offices. They expect the copy machine vendor, office products vendors, and office furniture vendors, as well as the local graphic artist, freelance writer, or whoever, to come visit their office to make their sales. There is usually a lot of leakage in ad-hoc purchasing through local chain stores and mail order. Often the administrators try to discourage this, but are only partially successful.

2.4.3 Competitive Forces.
The SB buyers understand the concept of service and support, and are much more likely to pay for it when the offering is clearly stated. There is no doubt that we compete much more against all the box pushers than against other service providers. We need to effectively compete against the idea that business should ever buy computers as plug-in appliances that don't need ongoing service, support, and training.

2.4.4 Communications.
One of the best places to reach the target SB is the local newspaper. Unfortunately, that medium is saturated with pure-price-only messages, and we'll have to make sure that our message is excellently stated. Radio is potentially a good opportunity. Our SB target buyers listen to local news, talk shows, and sports. Seminars are a good possibility with SB's. Employees are often happy to leave their normal routines for a day to learn something new.

2.4.5 Keys to Success.
The main key to success is making the business proposition clear. Many potential buyers would much prefer our offering to the box-only offerings of the chain stores and mail order sources, if only they knew the trade-off. Word of mouth is critical in this segment. We will have to make sure that once we gain a customer, we never lose them. We must always remember to sell the company, not the product. They have to understand they are taking on a relationship with AYWT Ltd, not just buying boxes. Boxes they can get cheaper elsewhere.

3.0 Marketing Plan Summary.
Allyourwishes Technology Ltd will change its focus to differentiate itself from box pushers and improve the business by filling the real need of small business and high-end home office for reliable information technology including hardware, software, and all related services.

3.1 Marketing Plan Pyramid.
Our main tactics include beefing up our service department and marketing service with mailers and promotions; improving training and marketing training; and offering seminars to targeted customer groups. There will also be a coordinated installed-base mailing program, and database management to turn mailings and seminars into leads and to turn leads into sales. Our advertising has to get better. We need to make sure that advertising serves our strategy, not just our corporate ego.

3.2 Marketing Strategy Summary.
The marketing plan includes our main strategies, tactics to implement each strategy, and programs to implement each tactic. These are explained in detail in the following section, beginning with the strategy.

3.2.1 Strategy: Emphasize service and support.
We must differentiate ourselves from the box pushers. We need to establish our business offering as a clear and viable alternative, for our target market, to the price-only kind of buying.

3.2.2 Strategy: Emphasize relationships.

Build long-term relationships with clients, not single-transaction deals with customers. Become their computer department, not just a vendor. Make them understand the value of the relationship.

3.2.3 Strategy: Specific market focus.

We need to focus our offerings on small business as the key market segment we should own. This means the 5-20-unit system, tied together in a local area network, in a company with 5-50 employees. Our values -- training, installation, service, support, and knowledge -- are more cleanly differentiated in this segment. As a corollary, the high end of the home office market is also appropriate. We do not want to compete for the buyers who go to the chain stores or mail order, but we definitely want to be able to sell individual systems to the smart HO buyers who want a reliable full-service vendor.

3.3 Marketing Tactics Summary.

The strategy pyramid shows the way tactics are linked to strategy and programs. There is an important set of tactics related to fulfilling our promise to the customer, generating good service and true expertise. Another set involves working much more with our established customer base, and a third set implements the idea of focusing on specific target markets.

3.3.1 Pricing Tactics.

We cannot compete on price in our market. The large chain stores are going to bury us if we try. We need to be able to come close on price, but we should be selling the company instead of the product.

3.3.2 Distribution Tactics.

We have two channels of distribution: in-store sales and outbound sales. For in-store sales, we are working throughout the new marketing strategy to develop targeted and focused marketing programs to generate walk-ins from our special target market segments, the small business and the high-end home office. For outbound sales, we need to get better at targeting leads and not pursuing leads that are not part of our target market segment.

3.3.3 Promotion Tactics.

This year we are going to focus our advertising better with our message, and add a lot more effort in seminar marketing and targeted mailings.

3.3.4 Tactics by Strategy.

Please note in the attached pyramid table how the different tactics link up and generate synergy. For example, the excellent training tactic included under the first strategy (emphasize service and support) will also help our implementation of the second and third strategies. Note also how much of our new marketing plan depends on good database management. We need to keep up our database and make it a true corporate asset.

3.3.5 Tactics by Product.

The most important product-oriented tactic is developing proprietary expertise, which means we have to beef up our ability to help our customers implement database management in multi-user settings in small business, and to implement fax and voicemail and internet facilities in the home office setting. We need to be able to differentiate with this expertise. Also, we need to improve our local area network and cross platform expertise.

3.3.6 Tactics by Market.

The product tactics divide into small business or home office as we look at local area networking and multi-user software expertise for small business, and fax and communications expertise for the high-end home office. The relationship-related tactics are similar for both segments, but the actual implementation (seminar, mailings, etc.) will vary for each of the main segments. We will offer different topics in seminars, different focuses on the mailings, for each of the segments.

3.4 Marketing Programs.

The most important collection of programs involves a new kind of marketing, seminar and mailing intensive, all of which falls under the general category of database-driven marketing.
We must market more to our established customers, because this is much less expensive than going into the open market to generate new leads.

3.4.1 Programs; Detail.

The table shows our planned programs in detail.

3.4.2 Programs; Expense Budget.

The most important programs are the mailing programs, with which we reach our target customers. These take a significant portion of total budget

3.4.3 Programs; Unit Sales Forecast.

As shown in the following table, we do not expect to be able to track sales very well. We will not easily be able to attribute sales to specific programs. Therefore, we have sales forecast more heavily into our general programs (sales force, advertising, for example) and less in the specific programs.

3.4.4 Programs; Sales Forecast.

The sales forecast reflects our notes in the previous section, about not being able to track sales into all programs. The largest sales generators, by far, are the sales force and advertising programs that we use to track general, unspecific sales.

4.0 Marketing Budget Summary.

The following marketing budget comes to a total of less than $480K. This is actually a decrease over the $485K we spent this year on the marketing budget. We believe we can get more effective marketing with less money, because we are managing the marketing better.

4.1 Budget by Type.

The largest single expenditure program is advertising, at $100K This is actually $40K less than we will have spent this year. The second largest is mailing, which is a priority because of its importance to our database marketing strategy.

4.2 Budget by Product.

The non-specific product spending amount to the largest total, $238K of the total $423K. The least is the training spending, at only $23K. The non-specific spending on product makes sense, because it is related to general training and development of our business expertise.

4.3 Budget by Market.

Our spending by market focus are mainly the non-specific spending, which is heavily influenced by advertising. Activities targeted for small business absorb much more of the budget than those looking at the high-end home offices, as the table shows.

4.4 Budget by Manager.

As the following table and chart show, the largest budget piece is $151K, which is almost entirely advertising budget, and managed by Fred.

5.0 Sales Forecast.

The more than $7 million sales forecast is shown in detail in the tables and charts to follow. This represents a 20% increase over the present year. We believe it is a conservative forecast, and we are sure we can make our numbers this year as a result of more effective marketing.

5.1 Sales by Product.

The more than $7 million sales forecast is shown in the following table and chart. As always, our largest single sales item is the sales of systems. The next largest item is the general, non-specific sales, which of course will also be mostly systems. The details follow.

5.2 Sales by Market.

Our most important market, by far, is the small business market. The sales forecast shown in the following table and chart is a superb reminder of why we need to focus on the specific target markets.

5.3 Sales by Manager.

As might be expected, Ken has by far the largest sales quota to manage. This is suited to our strategy of putting Ken in charge of the sales force, and tracking sales through the sales force. Details follow.

6.0 Marketing Organization.

AYWT Ltd is still a small company, despite our recent growth. Fred, the President, is responsible for general management. He specifically manages the advertising budget, but otherwise is responsible for sales and marketing as the head of the organization. Ken, our sales manager, is responsible for managing the in-house and the outbound sales forces. We have also put the mailing programs under Ken, because they must be carefully coordinated with the follow-up of the sales force. Sally, our marketing manager, is responsible for marketing programs including sales literature, trade shows, the catalog, etc. Charlie, who reports to Sally, will take the key role in the seminar marketing programs. Homer, who manages service, will also manage the marketing programs related to service.

7.0 Critical Issues.

7.1. Tracking and follow-up: will we have the discipline, as an organization, to track results of the marketing plan and make sure that we implement?

7.2. Market segment focus: how can we be sure we have the discipline to maintain the focus?

7.3. Saying no: can we say no to special deals that take us away from the target focus? Can we say no to unprofitable deals?

Notice that the marketing plan is cross-linked. It will specify which manager does what activity, plus cost per activity, resulting in cost per manager (activity), to which the managers salary can be added. Customers, typical customer profile and demographics are referred to where appropriate, enabling the reader to get an overview of market segmentation.

Summary
The marketing plan specifies how, why and where the product is to be sold. Furthermore it specifies who does what, when. By detailing all plans it enables a price to be put on these activities. This is of great help when making the budget.

15. Business plan

The business plan has been referred to before. It is the single most important document in attracting investors. However its importance is not only in attracting investors (including a bank, when the company needs a loan). It also functions as a "road map" which one always can refer back to, and is thus invaluable in keeping the company on track.

Classically entrepreneurs are supposed to practice their "elevator speech", explaining their business proposition in the time an elevator takes to travel from the 1st to the 10th floor. This may take the form of:

I have an idea. I can offer companies with up to 120 staff a system that will reduce their expenses with between 3% and 5%. Analysis shows that profit margins will be between 45% and 55%. I can reach the target group because I worked in that field for 5 years and know it well. Sales are by direct marketing.

The "elevator speech" does not mention gigabytes, server software or other details, it does not offer pie-in-the-sky. A business plan is similar, without going deep into product technicalities it outlines what the elevator speech says:

- What benefits it offers for the customer?
- What is the ROI?
- How is the customer to be reached?
- Which methods are to be used?

Obviously the business plan contains a bit more, as well. Typically the contents will be:

Executive Summary
Business Idea
Background*
Ownership and Company Structure
The Team: Leadership, Board of Directors, Accountants and Lawyers.
The Product
The Patent Situation*
Marketing Plan
Sales and Distribution
Competitors
Customers

Agreements and/or Alliances*
Budget
Investment Needs
Any Barriers
Profit and Exit

Those parts marked with an asterisk (*) are not always applicable to every business plan.

Venture Capitalists report that in 1999 and 2000 they were receiving 300 business plans per day. That means that the Executive Summary has to be very well written in order to get attention. It should be clear, concise and not one single word too long. Normally it is the part that is written last, since many experience that the process of writing the rest of the business plan helps formulate their ideas.

The business plan is a template. Much of the work covered in previous sections can simply be towed into position and afterwards reviewed to eliminate discrepancies, add missing details and ensure smooth reading. Variations on the basic template presented here exist. It is up to personal taste to find out which one suits you best.

The business plan normally starts with a cover page, stamped "Confidential", and containing a title and the name and address of the author. One may also wish to include the Mission Statement (13.4) on the title page and, according to length, a table of contents may be useful.

Executive Summary.
This is the "elevator speech" in writing. It contains the absolute essence of the business plan.

Business Idea
This is similar to the strategic business proposition described in 13. It includes a Porter-type analysis (13.1), a SGM (13.2) and SWOT analysis (13.3). It should start with a description of which problems the product solves and what advantages it offers to the customer, and the advantages it has over competing products/services.

Background
If applicable and if it adds to the prestige, then some background information can be added. For example if the invention was made in the research labs of a prestigious university and has won three major international prizes, then this can be documented here.

Ownership and Company Structure
This records the name and number of the company, the number of stock issued and their ownership, together with any other relevant information (e.g. accreditation, membership of professional organizations etc.). There should be a paragraph detailing how many others are employed, together with a projection about the company size in the future. Employee options and warrants may be detailed here, as it affects ownership issues.

It may also be relevant to add a paragraph about organization or mention any other special organizational aspects. This may be, e.g., if distribution is important that the company is located adjacent to major transport arteries, if it is a maritime company, that it is on the harbor front. Scientific companies may wish to mention that they lease premises in an incubator or science park etc. Note that there may be overlap with "Agreements or Alliances" (below).

The Team: Leadership, Board of Directors, Accountants and Lawyers.
The leadership will probably consist of the original inventors and entrepreneurs, together with any professional help, which has been bought or borrowed. This section should list their names, what their functions are, their affiliations and a brief CV of each one. It may be useful to make a matrix of their competence profiles in order to uncover any "holes". This shows the investor that the company is interested in being effective, as well as providing grounds for putting staff posts in the budget. It may be useful to give an indication that the entrepreneur is aware that, at least in the start, s/he will be working long hours for little money.

The Board of Directors is extremely important. A good board with 3-5 well-known and reputable directors will convince the investor that you have presented convincing arguments to competent and experienced people who, in turn, are able to steer the company and sell the product. They should be listed by name, together with their affiliation and perhaps a short description of their special field and competencies.

The names and addresses of the accountants and company lawyer come last.

The Product
A brief description of what the product is what it can do and how it differs from other products. If the product is not complete, then

milestones should accompany the development plan. Here product lifetime and expected frequency of buying may be relevant. It may also be the best place for pricing strategy. Note that price strategy can be different for different customer groups.

Pricing strategy.

Prices for new products can be calculated in two ways, either by adding up costs and putting profit (normally around 30%) on top, or finding out what the market can bear and charging that.

If a fast penetration strategy is planned, then introductory offers may be a good idea, and must be clearly labeled as such. Starting at a high price is risky as it may lead to a downward revision later, creating disappointment amongst the early customers.

Especially on the Internet, added value overshadows price. Most customers use the Internet to quickly find something which looks like a bargain, and then buy it more or less on impulse. However price is even less important if the convenience value is high, e.g. ordering last-minute perfume (with courier delivery) for a forgotten birthday. Customers shop at Amazon because it stocks four million titles, 200 times more than the largest physical bookshop, so many actually go there first.

If pricing is discussed here, then it is also relevant to discuss discounts, guarantee, follow-up and service strategy, help desk etc.

Drawings, blueprints etc. of the product can be attached as an appendix and should not be part of the business plan.

The Patent Situation
Here the IPR situation is briefly explained, including a description of competing patents. It is an excellent idea to include the results of searches performed by patent agents. These (copies of original letters), as well as any completed patents or patent proposals, should be attached as an appendix and should not be part of the business plan.

Marketing Plan
The marketing plan as described in section 14. Here possible product differentiation cam be described, for example if the same product, perhaps in different packaging, can be sold to different customer segments (see "customers" below). The marketing plan should also begin here to mention milestones.

Sales and Distribution

This section may include any details missing from he previous section. These may include any special advantages the company has, as well as special activities (Roll Out etc.). Price policy can be discussed here, if not already a part of the product description.

Competitors

There are always competitors (if not immediate, then at least potential). Stating that competitors do not exist will, unless it is an extremely special circumstance, make the business plan appear unrealistic. Indeed, if there are no competitors, then there is probably no market. Competitors should be listed together with a mini-SWOT for each one which realistically appraises the risks each one poses. This will lead to a suggested positioning strategy as to how to avoid them.

Customers

No two customers are the same. For example some will always go after the newest technology ("early movers"), whilst others are conservative and will not use a superior technology simply because it is new. Thus customers are broken down into segments according to different factors. These may be:

- Geographical factors e.g. country or population density (town or country-dwellers).
- Demographic factors, e.g. age, gender, income group, profession etc.
- Life style, e.g. environmentalists or techno-freaks.
- Behavior, e.g. way of using the product or frequency of use.
- Buying patterns, e.g., price-related or preference for certain trade marks.

This section should specify which customer segment is/are the primary target group(s) and which are the secondary, tertiary etc, if possible with a time scale (if not already mentioned in Marketing Plan).

Any Agreements or Alliances

This section specifies any agreements (further product development, media, marketing etc) which have been made with other companies, and any formal alliances (distribution, co-branding etc.) which have been signed, or are in the process of being negotiated. This may include suppliers, agents, franchising, resellers and retailers etc.

Budget
If the company has been running for some time, then the previous year's budget and accounts can be used. In principle this consists of:

- Net turnover.
- Change in inventory
- Other sources of income
- Raw and other supplies
- Other external costs (insurance etc.)
- Personnel costs
- Depreciation
- Other costs
- Earnings versus costs
- Disposition
- Tax

However it must be stressed that legal formats change with time and with country, so an accredited accountant is a must.

If the company is new then the budgets needs are estimated from the business plan. An accountant can help here, and there are also many types of accounting software available on the Internet and elsewhere. The running costs should ideally take cash flow into account.

Investment Needs
Investment needs follow logically from the budget. Obviously investment needs may continue over several years. Thus assumptions should be explicitly mentioned, which will result in "best case" and "worst case" investment projections.

Any Barriers
Barriers (if any) must be openly and honestly discussed, together with rescue scenarios. Often investors are willing to find extra cash for situations that have been foreseen, but hoped to be avoided. On the other hand, what investors really do not like, is unpleasant surprises. Unpleasant surprises may cause investors to suddenly withdraw their support, even where the extra amount may appear to be minimal.

Barriers can be divided into two types, external and internal. The most external could, for example, be changes in national law. Other external factors could already have been discussed under risks in the SWOT analysis, these could include that the factory burns down, competitors start marketing a cheaper product, the patent application fails, the major customer goes bankrupt etc. Internal factors may be that a key worker decides to leave, or the company cannot attract sufficient personnel of the right quality.

Profit and Exit

An investment should be a "win-win situation" for investor and company alike. Thus there must be a clear exit strategy from the start, a strategy which everybody knows about and explicitly approves.

Business plans can be from 2 to 30 pages long, with a large margin (2.5cm) so investors have space to make notes. The font size should not be under 11 point (max. 13, titles max. 16) with 1.5 line spacing. Tables and graphics should be very simple, preferably in monochrome because full color can appear garish, and accepted business plans will be photocopied anyway, so you may as well get a correct black/gray/white balance from the start. Pages should be numbered, and appendices clearly labeled.

Summary
The business plan is a clear and logically presented mapping out and overview of the work to be done and the needs to be met. As such it is invaluable to the entrepreneur and investor alike.

16. Attracting attention.

The difference between obscurity and the limelight is no accident - it takes a bit of show biz and sizzle. Personal inventiveness is the key, a natural part of the innovative entrepreneur.

Both the start-up and its product(s), should be marketed through as many channels as possible. At a minimum this is:

1. Web site.
2. Signature on e-mail.
3. Mail and web addresses on office stationary.
4. Mail and web addresses on visiting cards.

If there is money for TV spots, billboard advertising, or large ads in national newspapers, then your problems are luxury problems. Small start-ups do not normally have those kinds of resources, and thus must adhere to the maxim:

Marketing is an investment of limited size in one area, resulting in measurably higher income in another area.

So the problem is not to set the ball rolling, but rather to design a marketing project which is affordable, and which contains sufficient realizable checks and feedback mechanisms to make it possible to calculate almost exactly (remember marketing is not rocket science) how much revenue it has generated. Thus positioning the company is important, including choosing easily identifiable markets:

- Focus on the niche, "Position" your firm (high end, low price etc.).
- Live up to the image you built, be credible.
- Research the effectiveness of the effort.
- Develop expertise in the niche.

Today's competitive business environment demands focused efforts. It is very easy to get dragged into many diverse areas and not do any very well. The marketing budget can easily become a bottomless black hole into which money can be poured in a seemingly endless stream. Abdicating this responsibility to the "agency" is not the answer either. It is surprising how often "serious" marketers lack any kind of rational sense. They confuse familiarity with expertise, but they are not the same. This is because:

- We all are bombarded with advertisements
- We all comment about them
- We all love/hate some
- Advertising is ingrained in our life

Thus, many people have strong opinions but little knowledge. More money, time and effort are wasted this way than any other business activity. The entrepreneur must get to understand some of these issues as well as becoming used to working with professionals. How much money is enough? Most entrepreneurs spend too much or too little. Interestingly, once an effective campaign is found, entrepreneurs overspend 200-400% because there can't be no "too much of a good thing"; here are some ideas:

- Choose a percentage of sales or projected sales:
- Consumer oriented packaged goods 6-12%
- Big ticket consumer goods 4-8%
- Consumer services 5-8%
- Industrial equipment 2-4%
- For new products at the higher end, for established products, lower end.
- Set budgets yearly and review success regularly.
- Push up/down budgets if warranted.
- Set aside 10% of total budget for special opportunities.

Some questions the marketing department should be able to answer.

What percent of revenue is attributable to the top 10% and 20% of customers?
What is the firms' current share of the most profitable customers?
Does profit per customer increase after cross-selling
Are there any unprofitable customers, who's service costs outweigh revenue?
What is the average lifetime and value of the customer base?
What is the Return On Investment (ROI) for specific marketing campaigns?
Do specific campaigns increase customer satisfaction and loyalty?
Where are our customers and what is known about them?

Companies who do not have a unique technology are more dependent on Roll Out. Product (or company) roll out is important where the success of the business is dependent on quickly getting access to a large share of the market, and thus being able to dominate it, even in the absence of a dominating (i.e. unique) product. Here are some ideas around Roll Out:

- Plan promotion schemes
- Create "media events" where much free advertising can be created
- Try to anticipate a fad/trend
- Sponsor public activities
- Hold a one-company tradeshow
- Media relations are also very important, establish personal connections with specific writers/journalists, make their life easy and write the story, send in digital format, so they do not need to rewrite it.

Summary
Start-ups are highly dependent on publicity, especially free publicity, to spread information about them and their products as widely as possible. Resources for marketing are scarce and should be spent wisely.

16. Networking, leadership and other Critical Success Factors

The mention of networking may leave an unpleasant taste in your mouth. It conjures up images of Old Boys Club, people with funny handshakes and the Mafia. Common to all these phenomena is that the dead hand of monopoly lies over them. However the same leadership techniques will enable you to build up an invaluable network of contacts, based on openness, use, challenge and mutual respect.

How to develop a healthy blend of challenge and respect.

1. Encourage people to challenge your ideas, practices and assumptions.
2. Don't take challenge personally. Be confident enough to relate to the challenge as an issue, where you and the other person solve it together.
3. Welcome challenge as an opportunity to learn, not as a competition to be won or lost.
4. If someone disagrees, check that they really do disagree, or if they are just addressing a different side of the same issue.
5. Develop decision-making skills and use notes so that you can easily justify your decision later.
6. Avoid dualistic, black-and-white thinking. There are always alternatives.
7. Try to understand emotional processes. Conflict management rests often on emotional management.
8. Seek to express yourself clearly and listen well to others, they may be trying the same, but may not be so open or articulate as you.
9. Focus on the issue, not the person. Be as specific as possible and be prepared to admit that you may be wrong, or that your anxiety is based on a hunch. Not admitting this will create further problems.
10. Never put anyone in a situation in which they cannot save face. Many will risk (and even lose) their life to avoid embarrassment. This is especially important in cross-cultural situations.

Most people have inhibitions when starting to network. Try phoning first to someone you have met personally, explain that you know they are probably not "the person" you should talk with, but can they recommend anyone? You will be surprised how many people take it as a huge complement to be phoned up and asked for their opinion. You will also be surprised how many are willing to give you the benefit of their experience.

Of course, there is also a reverse side. At some point people will start ringing to you. This may not be the same person who you phoned to, but this third person may have got your name from that person. Of course, if it is your spouse's birthday party, then you may not be able to talk, but be courteous and arrange a mutually convenient time to ring back. Forgetting to reply can easily be taken as an insult. Remember that you 2 don't know each other, so it is easy for the requester to imagine all kinds of scenarios as to why you, perhaps deliberately, don't answer. So forgetting to reply will quickly get you cut out of that person's network (including those who know him/her).

A good network is immensely valuable. The majority of the heads of industry get enormous salaries not because of what skills they have, but because of whom they know. However networking needs the same skills as good leadership. A leader, who tells lies to the workforce and shrugs off their complaints, is justifiably unpopular and will not last long (or the best workers will leave).

This has led to the concept that the workforce works for you, and your network works for you. Both need the same approach. Your workforce does the things you can't do (or don't have time to do) and gets cash for this "favor". Your network also tells you the things you don't know (or don't have time to find out). OK, network contacts don't (often) get cash rewards, although even a little "thank you" note is surprisingly powerful.

Within start-ups the leadership strategy called "chance management" has become popular. Chance management is called such because the term is reminiscent of "change management". However change management should better be called "turnaround management", and chance management should properly be called "opportunity management". In its essence it is quite simple. In a start up many things happen which cannot be foreseen (indeed many are forced by quite unforeseeable outside factors). Therefore leaders should always increase their opportunities. When making a decision to do something, then, when that task has been completed, one should have a greater number of opportunities than before the task started. In any case opportunities should not become funneled down to a "all eggs in one basket" scenario.

Again, networking is similar, it should involve a growing number of contacts, never a reduction.

Handling cash is a critical success factor (CSF) and, if done poorly, it will cost you the company and part of this is borrowing. Borrowing is not a negative act, it is NOT a sign of weakness or a desperate act to save the business; nor a shameful "begging" exercise. Leveraging is a crucial vehicle for business growth a catalyst for expansion or a cushion for financial setbacks, plus an instrument for retaining equity. Borrowed capital should yield higher profits than its costs, the interest should be tax deductible and thus should not result in dilution, provided that you have collateral, and may be easier to obtain than equity. But, there are also drawbacks. You have to pay it back on time, interest servicing is a must, rates will fluctuate, and there may be limits to further borrowing. So, when you borrow, follow these "rules", especially if the lender is a bank (but even if not, the rules are mostly the same).

- Banking relationships are very important and should be nurtured:
- Deal with one bank for all your needs
- Build a trust relationship
- Involve the banker in your planning, don't give them any "surprises"
- Find a branch that has experience with small business
- Select a banker (loan officer) that understands you
- Open a line of credit and pay it back in order
- Remember that the banker you deal with is a person too, s/he has the same fears and problems as you have.
- Banks are in the business of lending to people who pay back, not in business to put you out of business.

Cash Reserves are another one of the CSFs in business and small businesses are almost always short of and cash.

- Most entrepreneurs underestimate the time it takes to make sales, the expenses, and surprises.
- Money buys time, especially at start-up, or when trouble strikes.
- When planning cash needs, give yourself at least a 25% margin of cash in addition to what you think you need.
- When you are in cash-flow trouble, borrowing is very difficult and, even if you get money, it may be very expensive.
- Plan from the start to have a plan "B" ready for the time when you may need cash in a hurry.
- Bad debts are real problems and in a successful business, there is no room for a "soft touch" credit policy. Customers are not customers if they don't pay their bills
- Extending credit is a crucial, yet delicate activity (not recommended).
- Credit handling in a right way multiplies business many times over.
- Casual treatment of business debts will bury the company.

- When extending credit to a customer, follow the rules of credit checking, open a file on the applicant, get at least 3 references, verify all information and make notes as you are checking
- Deny credit if there is any real evidence of habitual poor paying practice.
- When extending credit, set limits and carefully maintain surveillance of activity.
- Never provide credit to friends and family (providing "loans" to yourself is a criminal offence).

But, credit problems do occur and then you need to act promptly and decisively. If there is problem, follow these steps to collect. But if an account is more than 90 days overdue, then it should be turned over to a collection agency.

- The sooner you collect the more likely the success (over 1 year it is almost impossible).
- Personal contact by a "good" collector is very effective.
- It will take time (from 10 days to a year or more).
- This is especially serious if the account owes a significant amount with respect to sales.
- Most small businesses derive their revenues from a very few major accounts; this puts them into jeopardy when one of these customers gets into trouble.

There are many key business indicators that small companies use to avoid the "cash crunch". Small companies are much more fragile and can fail on a relatively small cash deficiency. The key financial indicators all relate to "liquidity" and for an entrepreneur, here is a brief list of what to pay attention to:

- Liquidity" is your ability to pay your bills. It is also called cash flow.
- The financial indicators are typically ratios such as the "current ratio" (from the balance sheet); here are some: Current Ratio = Current Assets/Current Liabilities >2:1. Note that Current Assets are cash-in-hand plus others easily convertible to cash assets.
- Cash position can be maintained by increasing current assets by borrowing long, adding equity in the form of cash, ploughing back profits and not paying dividends.

Most entrepreneurs are weak on the financial management side and this is especially the case for engineer entrepreneurs, however managing your money can not be abdicated to someone else, the responsibility is always yours. While it is difficult for most entrepreneurs to pay attention to the "numbers", ignoring financial statistics can (and will) be costly. Here are some of these important "numbers":

Balance Sheet
P/L Statement
Cash flow
Sales to profit ratio
Order backlog
Inventory status
Depreciation
NR and A/P
Debt financing status
Break-even charts for each LOB or product.

Excess inventories can cause many serious problems. Inventory ties up cash and can cause the firm to fail. Recommendations for inventory levels should be based on monthly sales and adjusted for order times. Approximations are:

- Hot sellers 45%
- Steady movers 30%
- Moderates 20%
- Slow sellers 5%

On the other hand, watch out for:

- Large carrying costs.
- Spoilage.
- Obsolescence.
- Warehousing costs.

Here are a bunch of other issues that could cause real grief:

- Not "building" a sales force is a deadly mistake, because nothing happens until a sale is made.
- Opening with the "Wrong Attitude" will create a negative first impression and these are crucial because people (customers) judge quickly
- "Perception is Reality", facts have little to do with anything.

- Risk management is an important issue, insurance is a major tool in this aspect.
- Many companies stay small because their owners never dare to think big. Expand wisely, the saying of "grow or perish" is a truism that will affect everyone sooner or later.
- Delegation to the wrong people (or lack of it) can be equally damaging
- Ignoring export opportunities
- Failure to recognize significant trends
- Timing in joining a new move to technology or developments such as the Internet
- Nepotism or other form of favoritism, where it is not clearly in the company's interest.

Believing one's "own advertisement" is a particularly easy and usually fatal mistake. The "ego" takes over and the entrepreneur begins really believe that s/he can do anything! This is usually first manifested in delegation, a sign of being strong enough to be able to "let go".

Delegation.

Delegation is being able to call upon a co-worker, explain what is wanted, and let them go, equipped with a reasonable budget and authority, to complete the task. Good delegation skills are a sign of mature authority. An early warning of bad management is bad delegation abilities, like giving a competent worker a badly thought out task, no means to accomplish it, and a good thrashing when it doesn't work.

Other signs of this problem brewing are:

- Expensive cars and lavish shows of "success"
- Absenteeism and arrogance
- Expansion into unrelated areas
- "Macho" attitude
- Ignorance of competition
- Maltreatment of employees
- Impatience and expectations can mount quickly, jumping the gun on any gradual process can seriously jeopardize its outcome.
- Counting profits before a sale is made
- Making financial commitments on expected profits (i.e. believing the spreadsheet plan as if it has happened).
- Neglecting personal finances.

- Many entrepreneurs mind the financial health of the business carefully while they neglect their own personal situation..
- Personal gain is a large motivator so keep your personal finances separate from the business, take profits out (as reasonably) to build your own wealth, use estate planners and stick to basic investment vehicles, consider tax issues, carry adequate insurance.
- Most successful entrepreneurs have spouse with large stable income, so personal issues have a way of adding trouble too (old saying, debt in the door - love out the window)
- Lack of exercise of personal control. Don't try to become friends with employees. You are the boss not friend! Choosing to be an "absentee owner" is a sure way to invite employee fraud, theft, general carelessness etc.

But, even the most dedicated owner must leave now and then; the six steps to "keeping the Boss in Control" are:

1. Leave clear instructions of where you are and how they can contact you when there is an important reason.
2. Leave a key person in charge while you are away.
3. Never leave on a regular basis for extended periods of time.
4. Audit your own operation periodically.
5. Build checks and balances to ensure that at least two people must "collaborate" to do something wrong.
6. Get rid of anyone who shows any dishonesty.

Summary
Personal style is important. Good leadership ethics and a healthy, honest and open style will enable the leader to manage both work (internal) and network (external) situations. Cash flow is the usual big CSF in small firms. Start-ups can additionally have problems with the entrepreneur's personality. Assuming profitability, bringing in professional help can alleviate both of these.

17. Encouraging entrepreneurial spin-offs.

In section 8 some characteristics of the innovative enterprise were described. However many established organizations are interested in becoming more innovative, or establishing innovative spin-off companies. The reason for this is that small innovative dynamic entrepreneurial companies, despite being high-risk, do give very good returns on investment.

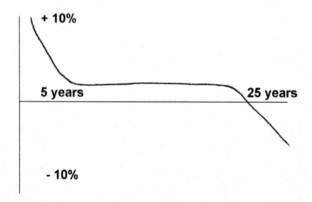

The above, idealized curve represents the total return to shareholders over time (years in that industry). It shows that entrants are the most lucrative portions of the market. This has given rise to the expression "attackers advantage, survivors curse". Thus many established players in the market wish to exploit this effect, either by becoming more innovative, or by establishing innovative subsidiaries. Some differences between the two types of organization are listed below:

	Operating organizations	Innovating organizations
Control	Focus on short-term performance	Set high long-term goals
	Watch costs	Focus on recruiting and developing human potential
	Hierarchy and control systems	Destroy to make room for innovations
Maintain	Stability and predictability	Accept ambiguities
	Reward success and punish failure	Tolerate honest failure

Clearly there have always been spin-offs. An example may be in the research labs of a large corporation. Corporate executives have decided to lay off scientists because the work of that certain research group should be terminated, because any products any products coming out of it will not be aligned with the corporate portfolio. Certainly at this point the scientists involved may decide that the product per se is valuable and set up their own company. The amount of badwill the spin off gets from the parent is quite variable, and in a clean break situation will probably revolve around patent rights and secrecy clauses.

The success of many spin-offs has meant that all but the most ossified of corporate executives now realize that it is reasonable to create benevolent spin-offs where the parent company grants a large amount of goodwill and invests heavily in the daughter company. In this way the parent can invest in the creation of new business, which is neither diversification nor divestment.

Diversification and divestment.

In the 1960s uncertainty amongst the "smokestack" industries led to widespread diversification. The strategy was that if you had a finger in many pies, then nothing much could go wrong. This went so far that many giant corporations ended up with divisions in rubber, in electronics, in chemicals, in steel, in coal etc. However it soon became obvious that quite different sets of skills were needed to profitably run each division.

This led to a process of divestment, where the new mentality dictated "do what you are good at". This shift meant that each industry had quite a narrow focus. It was built on the assumption that there only are a certain number of industries. Thus understanding and controlling these will lead to optimal performance.

The revolution of the 1990s opened up new business areas, it showed that it was possible to make business where there no previous industry or business existed.

The process involves increasing the field of vision by expanding business definitions. This focuses on creating new business, instead of just commercializing technology or developing products. The second step is to attract and motivate a team of exceptional performers with business-building experience, as well as recognizing the need for external linkages and flexible territories. This leads to the parent building a portfolio of investments. Recognizing that only a small percentage will be successful, a strategy of "try and prune" can be adopted, trying the market and cutting out if the expected results are not achieved.

This attitude involves radically changing some corporate assumptions, for example:

Corporate executives traditionally believe that	Spin off mentality believes that
one can judge market potential by analysis.	markets are unpredictable, leading to customer-led flexibility and early confirmation.
it is best to put management talent into ventures which are big and successful.	new ventures need the best management.
the likelihood of success should be very high before investing.	the likelihood of success is very low, so pruning quickly is the key to success.
shared ownership of ventures is an unacceptable risk.	shared ownership expands the "pie".
new ventures should quickly produce earnings and thus value for the parent.	market value can be significant before earnings are apparent.

The process of selecting areas and strategies can differ. However there are common elements.

1. **Preparation**. Existing business areas are documented, together with a value chain analysis (this can be comparative to the concepts of other companies).
2. **Generation**. These preliminary analyses are fed into a catalytic thought starter meant to unlock creativity.
3. **Shaping**. Promising concepts are used in a structured idea-generating workshop. This may be, e.g. "Idea Olympics", and run 2-3 iterations per potential growth area. At this stage a simple one-page description emerges for each new business concept. Ideas are screened for viability and opportunity.
4. **Preliminary development.** Detailed and practical business plans are developed for each idea. These are then prioritized and tested with the participation of industry expert.
5. **Validation.** Concepts are validated with key customers and the attractiveness of the value proposition determined.

Clearly, what comes out of the validation exercise can be re-fed into the cycle to polish the idea and develop new branches.

Summary
Industry entrants are more profitable than already existing players and also positively detract for the profitability of incumbents by creating new business opportunities. Thus established players may pursue a venture

policy by establishing innovative spin-offs, where the parent holds a significant part of the invested capital and provides part of the management team. Shortly, the innovative parent acts as an institutionalized venture capitalist.

18. Literature

The literature list is broken down into three parts:

- Recommended literature
- Cited and other useful literature
- Useful web links

Recommended literature	
Drucker, P.: Innovation and Entrepreneurship (1985), Butterworth Heinemann. ISBN: 0-7506-4388-9	The classical basis for understanding innovation.
McDonald, M.: Marketing Plans (1984), Butterworth Heinemann. ISBN: 0-7506-4116-9	Probably the best book ever written on the theory and practice of marketing
Mellor, R. B.: The Web Managers Handbook (2003), Globe. ISBN: 87-7900-190-4	Essential for those who want to do business on the Internet

Cited and other useful literature	
Barrow: The essence of small businesses (1998), Financial Times/Prentice Hall. ISBN: 0-13-748641-3	A little old, but still a useful and practical guide.
Bickerstaffe, G. (ed.): Mastering management (1997). Pearson Education. ISBN: 0-273-62729-5	The management bible.
Boisot, M.. Knowledge Management (1998). Oxford University Press. ISBN: 0-19-829607	An excellent and innovative book putting knowledge and knowledge assets on the center stage.
Cameron, R. and Neal, L.: A concise economic history of the world (2003). Oxford University Press. ISBN: 0-19-512705-6	An interesting background about economic evolution.
DeBono, E.: Serious creativity (1995). Harper Collins. ISBN: 0-00-637958-3	A collection of DeBono's ideas in one book.

Dobson, S. and Palfreman, S.: Introduction to economics (1999). Oxford University Press. ISBN: 0-19-877565-2	A general introduction to economics.
Drucker, P.: Management challenges for the 21st century (1999), Butterworth Heinemann. ISBN: 0-7506-4456-7	Drucker looking into the future.
Perman, R. and Scouller, J.: Business economics (1999). Oxford University Press. ISBN: 0-19-877523-5	The standard textbook detailing business and economics.
Phillips: E-business strategy (2003), McGraw-Hill. ISBN: 0-07-709837-4	Some interesting cases. Can be used as a supplement to The Web Managers Handbook"
Porter, M.: Competitive Advantage, creating and sustaining superior performance (1985). Free Press N.Y. (edition of 1998) ISBN: 0684841460	A classic and bestseller.
Stacey, R.: Complexity and creativity in organizations (1996). Berrett-Koehler. ISBN: 1-881052-89-3	Creativity and change in organizations.
Smith, A.: An inquiry into the nature and causes of the wealth of nations (1776). Prometheus Books; (1991) ISBN: 0879757051	The root of economics

Useful web links	
www.europa.eu.int	The EU
europa.eu.int/celex	The EUs database about laws, tractates, international agreements etc. Requires subscription.
Europa.eu.int/eclas/	EU central library.
Europa.eu.int/eur-lex	Laws in power in the EU.
Europa.eu.int/citizens	Citizens and companies rights in the inner market
Europa.eu.int/business	The EUs dialog with the business world.
Europa.eu.int/eurostal.html	European statistical office

Eurodic.echo.lu	Translations of terms and abbreviations
euror.eu.int	The EUs electronic publication archive
Europarl.eu.int/r/dors/oeil/en/	The European parliament observed! (free and good).
www.cordis.lu	Database about technological research and development in the EU and partner countries
Simap.eu.int	Information about offers open to bidding
www.ted.eur-op.eu.int/index2.htm	Public contracts in the EU countries
Mkaccdb.eu.int	EU: Import and export control.
www.ispo.cec.be	Promoting the information society.
Eurofound.ie/information/emire.html	The EU market for work and human resources.
www.eu-lex.com	Association of independent lawyers (not to be confused with Europa.eu.int/eur-lex). Subscription needed
www.tradeport.org	Trade information, better than the CIA.
www.corporateinformation.com	Business intelligence.
www.morebusiness.com	Excellent source of standard contracts, forms etc.
www.uk-business-formations.co.uk	Set up your company here.
www.leadertoleader.org	On business tactics and strategy
www.pwcglobal.com	Download their Information Guide series
www.undpo.org	UN development program.
www.unicc.org	International computing center
www.unido.org	UN organization for industrial development
Worldbank.org	IBRD (International Bank for Reconstruction and Development)
www.imf.org	International Monetary Fund.
www.afdb.org	African Development Bank
www.adb.org	Asian Development Bank
www.oecd.org	OECD (Organization for Economic Cooperation and Development)
www.coe.fr	Council of Europe.

www.ifad.org	International Fund for Agricultural Development
www.intracen.org	International Trade Center
www.wto.org	World Trade Organization.
www.ecb.org	European Central Bank

19. Appendix A: R U E-Ready?

This is a self-evaluation about your readiness for opening an online store. It may also serve as measurement of the potential degree of success based upon market data and experience. This evaluation does not guarantee results but should be used in conjunction with other forms of guidance and advice. This quiz is reprinted with permission of intercollege.org.uk.

1. What is the "uniqueness" of your product or service that you intend to sell on the Web?.

A	B	C	D
Commodity, universally available	Available only from a small number of suppliers	Available only in my region	Completely unique and available only from me

2. Are you adding the ability to take orders to an existing Web site or creating your commerce-Web site for the first time?

A	B
Adding	New

3. Do you have a Merchant I.D.? (the bank registration number for credit card processing.)

A	B
Yes	No

4. Do you have resources available to design your Web site? (These could be in-house staff or out-sourced personnel).

A	B
Yes	No

5. Are you prepared to make a reasonable financial investment (at least 10,000 GBP)?

A	B
Yes	No

6. Are you willing to dedicate additional resources to promote your Web site?

A	B
Yes	No

7. Do you have plans, procedures, relationships, etc. to fulfill customer orders ?

A	B
Yes	No

8. Are there any business associations that can or will provide support for your online efforts?

A	B
Yes	No

9. Are there any other companies in your industry who have been successful in selling on the Web?

A	B	C	D
No others on the Web	Yes, they're on the Web, but don't take orders	Yes, they're taking orders on the Web, but with little success to date	Yes, they're taking orders on the Web and are successful

10. What is your priority for integrating your Web store with your business accounting system?

A	B	C
Not a priority	Plan to do this when business dictates	I must be able to do this before my store goes online

11. Does your Internet Service Provider (ISP) have the capability to assist you in your efforts to open a Web store?

A	B	C	D
Yes	No	Not yet chosen	Don't know

12. According to your customer profiles, what is their preference for buying products or services similar to yours on the Web?

A	B	C	D	E
They don't at all	They buy other things but not these	They are just starting to purchase	They are occasional Web shoppers	They are loyal Web shoppers

13. Your products or services are recognized name brands.

A	B
True	False

14. Do you have a service or product catalog business already ?

A	B
Yes	No

15. Are there active Internet newsgroups, discussion groups, and/or forums that discuss products or services that you intend to offer for sale?

A	B	C
No	Don't know	Yes

16. According to the demographics or profile of your Web customer, are they on the Web and do they have the means to purchase online (e.g., credit card, business purchase order, electronic cash)?

A	B	C
Yes	No	Don't know

17. Do your products require the customer to touch or feel them prior to the shopper's first purchase?

A	B
Yes	No

18. What level of product customization do you offer?

A	B	C	D
None	Less than half of my business is custom	More than half of my business is custom	Business is entirely custom

19. Your business area is dominated by a large number of small businesses?

A	B
True	False

20. Do you have staff to interact with your on-line customers and are they computer-qualified?

A	B
Yes	No

21. What amount of your business is from repeat purchases ?

A	B	C
None	Some	A great deal

Are You Ready? Scoring

Question	Points for your answer					Your Score
	A	B	C	D	E	
1	0	3	5	7		
2	3	1				
3	5	0				
4	5	2				
5	4	2				
6	1	0				
7	1	0				
8	3	0				
9	1	3	5	7		
10	5	5	0			
11	10	0	5	3		
12	0	4	7	10	15	
13	5	0				
14	15	7				
15	0	1	3			
16	15	0	7			
17	0	7				
18	7	8	9	12		
19	5	3				
20	10	0				
21	1	3	7			

Your overall score: _____

Web Store e-Readiness Index Score	
You're more than ready and will likely be successful. You have spent the appropriate amount of time planning and seem to understand the limitations of selling online.	**151-184**
You're ready and seem to have most items in place for launching your store. You may want to evaluate your answers to see if there are any areas for improvement.	**121-150**
You should be ready soon. You may want to evaluate your answers to see if there are any areas that you have missed in your planning.	**86-120**
You've got some work to do before you open your store. You seem to be missing critical areas in your planning and should re-evaluate your answers.	**51-85**
You are not ready to open and may be overestimating your ability to open your store. You should re-evaluate your answers before you move forward.	**20-50**

20. Index.

A

accounts;68
active investment;40
added value;66
advertisements;71
alliances;67
assets, current;76

B

badwill;80
bank loan;45
barriers;68
barriers to entry;47
benchmarking;10
blueprints;66
Board of Directors;36;65
borrowing;74
budget;65;68
business angel;34;36
business innovator;28
business plan;63;69;82

C

cash crunch;76
cash flow;39;68
cash reserves;75
cash-in-hand;76
channels;70
Co.;45
co-branding;67
collateral;46
competitors;67
Confucius;15
Connect;34
copyright;11
creative destruction;13
creative imitation;39
creativity;18;82
credit;76
Critical Success Factors;48;73
CSF;*See* Critical Success Factors
customers;66;67

D

DeBono, E.;21
delegation;78
demographics;67
depreciation;77
dilution, of capital;42
discounts;66
discovery;9
distribution;67
diversification;81
divestment;81
Drucker, P.;16
due diligence;41

E

Eddison. T.;28
elevator speech;63
entrepreneur;13;31;63;79
entrepreneurship;13
equity;75
Ethernet;24
exit;69

F

FFF
    Friends, Family and Fools;37
franchising;67
Friedman, M.;15
Fuqua, J.B.;13

G

goodwill;81
guarantee;66

H

help desk;66
holding company;45

I

ICT;25
Inc.;45
incentives;9
incubator;34
industry attractiveness;47
Information Technology;25
Initial Public Offering;27
innovation, horizontal;6
innovation, incremental;6
innovation, radical;6
innovation, vertical;6
insurance;79
interest group;48
Internet Service Provider;24
invention;10;11
inventory;68;77
Investor;34
investor relations firms;40
IPO;*See* Initial Public Offering
IPR;10;11;35;66;*See* Intellectual Property Rights
ISP;24

K

Kondratieff, N.;16

L

LAN;23
Letter of Intent;41

Limited Company;44
Limited Liability Company;44
liquidity;76
LLC;*See* Limited Liability Company
Ltd.;45

M

Malthus, T.;15
management, chance;52;74
management, conflict;73
management, just-in-time;8
management, opportunity;52;74
management, risk;78
management, turnaround;74
manager, Adventurer;33
manager, Farmer;33
manager, Hunter;33
manager, Turnaround, Visionary;33
manager, Warrior;33
Marco Polo;31
margin;75
marketing plan;52;53;66
media;72
Mellor, R. B.;33
mergers and acquisitions;37
micro-business;23
milestone;41;66
Mission Statement;50
modem;24
monetarism;15

N

NASDAQ;5
network;74
Non Disclosure Agreement;41
Novell;23

O

Object-Oriented Programming;23
options;41

P

patent;35;63
PC;23
penetration strategy;66
Phillips;11
PLC;45;*See* Product Life Cycle
Porter, M.;47
pre-seed capital;37
pricing strategy;66
product champion;28
Product Life Cycle;32
profit;69
proof of concept;37
prototype;35

R

RAM;23
resellers;67
retailers;67
Return On Investment;71
Ricardo, D.;15
ROI;*See* Return On Investment
roll out;71

S

Say, J-B;12;15
Schlumpeter, J.;16
science parks;37
screening;34
seed capital;37
service;66
SME;23;34
Smith, A.;15
spin-off;27;79
sponsor;34
Strategic Group Mapping;48
strategy;47
SWOT;49
syndication;40

T

Term Sheet;41
Time To Market;39
trade secret;12
trading, general;44
trading, sole;44
TRS, Total Return to Shareholders;80
TTM;52
TTM, *See* Time To Market;39
turnover;68

U

UNIX;23

V

venture capital;34
venture capitalist;82

W

WAN;23
warrant;41

Z

Zeiss;27